the scent of
pomegranates
and rose water

the scent of pomegranates and rose water

Reviving the Beautiful Food Traditions of Syria

**Habeeb Salloum,
Leila Salloum Elias,
and Muna Salloum**

ARSENAL PULP PRESS

VANCOUVER

ARSENAL PULP PRESS
Suite 202 – 211 East Georgia St.
Vancouver, BC V6A 1Z6
Canada
arsenalpulp.com

The publisher gratefully acknowledges the support of the Government of Canada and the Government of British Columbia (through the Book Publishing Tax Credit Program), for its publishing activities.

Arsenal Pulp Press acknowledges the xʷməθkʷəy̓əm (Musqueam), Skwxwú7mesh (Squamish), and səl̓ilwətaʔɫ (Tsleil-Waututh) Nations, speakers of Hul'q'umi'num'/Halq'eméylem/hən̓q̓əmin̓əm̓ and custodians of the traditional, ancestral, and unceded territories where our office is located. We pay respect to their histories, traditions, and continuous living cultures and commit to accountability, respectful relations, and friendship.

The author and publisher assert that the information contained in this book is true and complete to the best of their knowledge. All recommendations are made without the guarantee on the part of the author and publisher. The author and publisher disclaim any liability in connection with the use of this information. For more information, contact the publisher.

Design by Oliver McPartlin
Arabesque decoration designed by Freepik
Photography by Tracey Kusiewicz/Foodie Photography (FB: Foodie Photography; IG & TW: @foodie_photo)
Food styling by Tracey Kusiewicz and Carol Jensson
Props styling by Tracey Kusiewicz
Ceramics provided by Jackie Frioud, Nima Stoneware, Gailan Ngan, Hide Ceramic Works

Editing by Shirarose Wilensky
Copy editing by Anumeha Gokhale
Proofreading by Alison Strobel

Printed and bound in Canada

Library and Archives Canada Cataloguing in Publication:
Salloum, Habeeb, 1924–, author
The scent of pomegranates and rose water : reviving the beautiful food traditions of Syria / Habeeb Salloum, Leila Salloum Elias, Muna Salloum.
Issued in print and electronic formats.
ISBN 978-1-55152-742-0 (hardcover).—ISBN 978-1-55152-743-7 (PDF)
1. Cooking, Syrian. 2. Cooking, Syrian—History. 3. Cooking—Syria—History. 4. Cookbooks. I. Elias, Leila Salloum, author II. Salloum, Muna, author III. Title.

TX725.S9S25 2018   641.595691   C2018-901949-2
                                              C2018-901950-6

Contents

· · · · · · · · · · · ·

A Brief History of Syrian Cuisine

Habeeb Salloum
Leila Salloum Elias
Muna Salloum

The culinary art of the Greater Syria region, the area known in Arabic as *bilaad al-shaam,* which today encompasses Syria, Lebanon, Jordan, and Palestine, took shape century after century, as culture after culture flowed through the Middle East. From the misty days of early civilizations until our times, Hittites, Akkadians, Assyrians, Eblaites, Egyptians, Persians, Greeks, Romans, Armenians, Byzantines, Ottomans, and modern Europeans all left traces of their foods. Diverse ethnicities such as Arabs, Assyrians, Kurds, Armenians, Yazidis, the Syriac-speaking peoples, and religious groups such as Muslims, Christians, Jews, and Yazidis, have all contributed to the depth and richness of Syrian cuisine.

The cuisine of Greater Syria reached its epitome after the turn of 7th century, during the Umayyad and Abbasid dynasties, when the Arab-Islamic Empire reached its zenith. The great cosmopolitan cities of the empire became centers for the development of the culinary arts. Arabic cooking manuals originating in Baghdad, Aleppo, Damascus, Cairo, Murcia, Granada, and Seville provide evidence of a great food culture. Documents from medieval Arabic manuals of market inspectors indicate that nutrition and hygiene went hand in hand with how people ate, sold, and regulated their food. The 600 or so recipes in the earliest extant Arabic cookbook, from 10th-century Baghdad, give us a window into the meals of the upper echelons of society, from noble to caliph. Three hundred years later, three Arabic cooking manuals from Baghdad, Aleppo, and Cairo, and two from Murcia

7

(Arab Spain) include recipes similar to the 10th-century ones, proving the Arabs brought their food with them wherever they went.

With expansion came contact with new peoples, new ideas, and new foods. Some dishes were adopted, some were transformed, and many were created with new ingredients. One good example is the pre-Islamic simple sweet snack of the 6th century called *hays*, which was originally made only with dates, dried curd, and clarified butter. By the 13th century, it had evolved into dates, pistachios, walnuts, almonds, and toasted sesame seeds, sprinkled with finely ground sugar. What helped immensely in the adoption and development of new foods and dishes in modern-day Syria was that Aleppo and its sister city Damascus were at the western end of the Silk Road, the pathway of trade between the Far East and Europe for some 4,000 years. No less important was the Incense Route, on which the perfumes and spices brought by sea on Arab *dhows* from the Far East and India to southern Arabia were transported overland. During the peak of creative development of medieval Arab food culture, the cooks behind the scenes in the kitchens of the palaces of the caliphs and emirs, vied with each other, devising appetizers (*bawaarid*) and entrées, to sweets and beverages. In those great palaces of the past, scores of kitchen help prepared lavish feasts and banquets. Although the earliest extant Arabic cookbook credits several caliphs, nobles, musicians, physicians, and cooks—all male—for certain fabulous recipes, there are occasional references to female cooks too. For example, the slave, Bid'a, was known for her sour stew called *sikbaaj*, appetizers, and unparalleled sweets. Her mentor, 'Arib, was renowned for her own dishes, and even chastised a governor, at one point, for not recognizing her culinary skills. Women cooked, but in a patriarchal society, men got the credit.

And with these new dishes with sophisticated new flavors, a new poetic genre emerged in Arabic literature. At one banquet, guests used flowing words to set asparagus, *hareesa* (see p. 197), and *qataayif* (see p. 309) in poetry. Sometimes the recipe became poetry, such as famed Baghdadi musician Ishaq al-Mawsili's description of how to make *sambousek*, little savory pies.

Oh you who asks about the most tastiest of foods,

You've asked the most qualified of men to conclude.

You resolve upon meat that is red and not tough;

Pound it with its fat, not a lot but enough.

An onion that's cut in rounds in it is thrown

And very green cabbage that's been freshly grown.

After, throw in the rue, an amount that is plentiful

And cinnamon and coriander an amount of a handful.

Then somewhat of cloves after this do you add

And ginger and pepper of good quality not bad

And cumin a handful and murri but a slight

And a measure of two handfuls of salt from Palmyra.

Then pound them, my lord, pound them a lot,

Then kindle a fire for them, a fire that's hot.

Place it all in a pot and over it pour water,

Then place over it a lid to form as a cover.

When it appears that the water is gone and is few,

And the fire beneath it has dried it all up too,

Then roll it, if you wish, in dough that is thin,

Then seal up the edges in what you've put the meat in.

Or take an even portion of dough, if you fancy,

Rub with the hands softly and gently.

Roll it out with the rolling pin until it is round,

Then with fingernails scallop the edges around.

Into the frying pan pour in oil that is good,

Then fry them, fry well, this understood.

Put them in a bowl that is delicate and dainty;

In its middle is mustard, its pungency tasty.

Eat them, a food delicious with mustard aflurry;
Indeed, this is the best for those in a hurry.

As well, physicians became involved in how, when, and what to eat and drink under the auspices of their caliph patrons. Overindulgence in food would lead to an unhealthy body and disposition, which would compromise the leadership of the vast empire. Most caliphs ate under the watchful eye of a personal physician at their table, who advised which dishes were conducive to the caliph's health and even how their food should be chewed. If, for example, Harun al-Rashid's physician could not be found, the caliph's guards would go from house to house, to return him to the palace.

Even the cookbook authors included physicians' advice on the health benefits of certain dishes or ingredients. These Arabic cooking manuals include remedies for certain ailments or illnesses, as well as the dos and don'ts of drinking water. Instructions on the proper use of kitchen utensils were also given, with examples of how to clean pots, as well as notes on hygiene. One such directive, for the stew of oranges and meat (*naranjeeya*), stipulates that the person who peels the orange should not be the same one who squeezes it.

By the end of the 11th century, *bilaad al-shaam* fell victim to the Crusades, followed by the invasion of the Mongols in the 13th century, who devastated the region and destroyed the existing civilization. Mamluk rule ended the Crusader wars and brought some stability to the region. Finally, in 1516 CE, the Ottoman occupation began. Greater Syria was no longer "great" but rather under the jurisdiction of foreign rule.

The first two centuries of Ottoman rule were somewhat stable. However, from the 18th century until the beginning of WWI, Greater Syria experienced economic decline and poverty, corruption, oppression, high taxes, and even famine.

During the 18th century, natural disasters such as drought, hail, and torrential rains plagued the region. In 1759, an earthquake damaged the region's agriculture yields. Swarms of locusts and a mice infestation affected Damascus and Aleppo and the surrounding grain-producing fields. The Aleppo region received inadequate rainfall, so grain had to be imported from the neighboring provinces and beyond. In the second half of the century, winters were extremely cold and summers, hot and dry. In 1750 and again in 1764, a horrendous heat wave dried wells, fresh springs, and one of the major canals on the outskirts of Damascus in the Ghouta, where olives and fruit ordinarily grew plentifully.

In times of food shortages and famine, Ottoman officials manipulated food supplies, stockpiling sheep and grains and tripling the price of meat and flour. The state took meat and wheat to feed the Imperial Janissaries and supplement the sultan's kitchen. The former Ottoman measures of price-fixing and market supervision were now under the influence of local factions, governors, and families.

By the mid-19th century, the once-powerful Ottoman Empire was deteriorating, labeled by Tsar Nicholas I as the "the sick man of Europe." Hardship continued, and in the late 19th century, times were getting worse for most Syrians. There was, however, some prosperity in Aleppo, Damascus, and Mount Lebanon. The upper-class families of Damascus took the lead in literature and art, simply because they had the means to eat and enjoy life, whereas, at times, laborers and the poor had to be satisfied with a loaf of bread. In this century, Greater Syria, once prosperous and self-supporting, was caught in the vicissitudes of its surroundings, conquered by the Egyptians and then again by the Ottomans, and subjected to the whims of interfering foreign powers. By now, it was only the small ruling class that lived well.

Rich or poor, Muslim or Christian, most Syrians in the 18th and 19th centuries followed the same social and familial customs and traditions of previous generations. The father was the respected head of the family who made all major decisions and had the final word. It was not uncommon to hear a woman refer to her husband with the endearment *taaj raasee* (crown on my head). Today, such terms are long gone, as women have come into their own. Although traditional family values and structure remain, family dynamics have evolved in this new modern age in which both men and women pursue higher education, enter the workforce, share family responsibilities, and build a future together.

The mother's important role within the family was to teach her children the social rules of etiquette and behavior as well as religious traditions. The mother was respected and honored; her children would greet her in the morning with a kiss on her hand. Women took care of all household matters, including cooking. They made sure that whatever was needed to prepare a meal was on hand, checking the dry ingredients in the *bayt al-mouni* (pantry) daily. The mother was responsible for putting breakfast, lunch, and dinner on the table, in a communal effort with her daughters and other female relatives in the house.

Women of the countryside also worked with their husbands in the fields, the material backbone of rural life, along with their children and other family members who resided with them. They helped grind the wheat, bring fresh water from the spring, collect firewood, and harvest. They also made sure the clay *qawara* that stocked their wheat and barley were always filled.

In the 18th and 19th centuries, upper-class urban families lived in houses that were usually passed down to them over generations. The famous courtyard houses of Damascus and Aleppo, most of which are preserved today as restaurants and boutique hotels serving traditional dishes of the past, were conducive to a number of family members living together, both before and after marriage. The ancient wooden doors concealed the magnificence of an interior courtyard with a central fountain and the Syrian-style mosaics and tiles of the home within.

Outside the houses, in the narrow streets of the city, produce vendors walked their horse and buggies, selling their wares and shouting, "*Kousa, Kousa! Basal, basal! Khiyaar, khiyaar!*" (Marrow/squash/zucchini! Onions! Cucumber!) during the early-morning hours. Mothers would send their children out to purchase the fresh vegetables and fruit for that day's meals. Garlic was in high demand during this period, not only as a condiment but as a means to stop food from spoiling. In almost every quarter in Damascus there were shops and stalls where grocers sold their fresh produce; other stalls sold pickled foods, mustard, vinegar, dried pulses and grains, spices, and sweets. The Bedouin and the rural farmers in the nearby villages produced and sold fresh milk and homemade cheese daily. If the plan for the day was to make kibbeh, the wife would give instructions to purchase fresh meat and onions as soon as the market opened. Bakeries opened early to supply the city folk with their daily bread. Special breakfasts involved a trek to the local bakery for fresh *manaqeesh* (a round flatbread topped with za'atar, cheese, or ground meat). Various types of nuts were also available—raw or freshly roasted; walnuts and hazelnuts were less expensive since they grew just outside Damascus, whereas, pistachios and almonds a bit pricier because they were brought in from the north of the country. Pine nuts and sesame seeds were also costly.

While the women tended to their daily duties at home, the men went to work. For those who could not leave their businesses for a lunch break, a meal was delivered to them, usually by one of their sons. Otherwise, the quarter had small eating places for a late breakfast or lunch of chickpeas or fava beans. Tea or coffee was always available and could be delivered right to the workplace. For those who went home for lunch, a full meal would be ready. This would be the main meal of the day. It was a common practice to take a nap after the meal, before returning to work.

If the husband worked all day and returned home late, his wife would prepare a full dinner after having fed the younger children earlier. In this instance, the husband would dine by himself or accompanied by his sons older than ten. Of course, this may have differed from household to household, but tradition usually took precedence.

With family, came honor. Two major traits, inherent to the Arab code of honor (*murou'a*) that originated in Arab tribal society, were hospitality and generosity. The 18th-century Scottish physician and naturalist, Alexander Russell, aptly observed that peasants and the poor would freely offer a portion of their homely fare to strangers. In *Travels in Syria and the Holy Land*, John Lewis Burckhardt writes that when a visitor alights at any house "a mat will be immediately spread for him, coffee made, and a breakfast or dinner set before him." Burckhardt and Russell's remarks reflect the generations-old Syrian custom of treating guests honorably and providing for them. Despite their poor conditions, Syrians in the 18th and 19th centuries continued the all-important tradition of hospitality that each family lived by. The best food was put on the table for the guest, according to the centuries-old expression: "*Yaa dayfunaa, la-wajadunaa, nahnu al-duyoof, wa anta rabb al-manzilee*" ("Oh, our guest! If you find us, we are the guests and you are the lord of the house"). In times of plenty or hardship, this mainstay of Arab culture was maintained.

Both Christians and Muslims celebrated religious holidays on a grand scale. For the two major holidays in Islam, the end of Ramadan (Eid al-Fitr) and the Feast of Sacrifice (Eid al-Adha), and Easter and Christmas for the Christians, the best meals and sweets were prepared to pass out to guests who came to offer their holiday greetings. Meat dishes graced the tables of those who could afford it; for the poor and peasants who usually subsisted on *laban* (yogurt), bread, pulses, and barley, a holiday may have been the one day in the year that meat was offered. When times were good, the well-to-do families of Aleppo and Damascus had a full diet of meats and poultry, cooking oils and butter, fresh produce, spices, and even prepared sweets from local bakers. Yet despite the high meat prices in the 18th century, Damascus's upper classes paid to have it, since it maintained the appearance of a high social status. For the poor, however, meat signified luxury, so instead they subsisted on food they grew themselves, such as wheat, lentils, and chickpeas.

This cookbook features dishes from the 18th and 19th centuries that were prepared by both the affluent and the poor in the kitchens of *bilaad al-shaam* in times of plenty, as well as insufficiency. However, these recipes that are so ingrained in people's lives in this region have not had their chance to be introduced to the world—until now. The recipes in this book reach beyond the popular, to include dishes from an era about which so little has still been written. Their preservation may well be a form of nationalistic and cultural identity; a reminder, that despite war and occupation, political machinations and shifting borders, natural disasters and economic fluctuations, these dishes have been handed down for generations, a part of a family's legacy; a nexus between the past and the present.

In the rural areas of Greater Syria in the 18th and 19th centuries, people sustained their existence with dishes based upon what they could grow and raise, what was available by season, and what they learned from their parents and grandparents. The inhabitants of the major cities took on the role of preserving, what were once the dishes of nobility, leading Aleppo and Damascus to become the focal points of distinctive food culture in Syria.

What has made Aleppo's food culture so special? The city's dishes draw inspiration, not only from the wealth of its history and the diversity of its ethnic communities, but also from the verdant countryside. The herds of fat-tailed Awassi sheep, fields of nuts, orchards of olive, and fruit trees produce signature ingredients such as pomegranates, Aleppo pepper, and pistachios. No one dining on grilled meat flavored with pomegranate molasses or buried in yogurt, barbecued meatballs with black cherries, a green wheat pilaf called freekeh, or on one of the many, many unique varieties of kibbeh will ever forget the world-class cuisine of this city. The food of Aleppo is more heavily seasoned than in any other part of Syria. Yogurt is a component of many dishes, and each meal usually includes a variety of meat preparations. Aleppans pay attention to detail, combinations of flavors, and elegance of presenting their food.

Aleppo may be recognized as the gastronomic capital of Syria, but about 225 miles south, the Damascenes take exceptional pride in their own food—a cuisine that has developed over centuries. The best place to taste traditional Damascene cuisine, other than in someone's home, is in the people's eating places. The large hotels and fine dining restaurants cater to foreign visitors and the upper echelon of Syrian society. However, in the heart of Old Damascus, the ovens diffuse the enticing aromas of thyme and cheese and the seductive fragrance of steaming *yakhnee* (stew) as a testimony to the city's magnificent variety of home-cooked meals. You can enjoy authentic home-style Damascene and Syrian cuisine in the Old City in the newly renovated courtyard (*daar*)-style restaurants, with trickling fountains and traditional Syrian decor. And don't forget to finish with a few puffs on the hookah, a perfect finale to a perfect meal.

Generally speaking, many Syrians today are unaware or have little interest in this great culinary tradition of the glorious past. Habeeb and Muna still remember their conversation with the Manuscripts Catalogue Librarian at the Assad Library in Damascus. When Muna asked if there were any new additions to the Arabic cooking manuals from the early medieval period to the 19th century, he looked at her stunned. "What do you mean? There are recipe books from that far back?" Muna quickly explained there was a history of at least 1,000 years of cookbook writing in the Arab world and eloquently gave examples of the luxury foods that appear in those books. His response: "*Wallah* (Really)? They had more than baba ganoush?" His thoughts were echoed by the Syrian Lebanese owner of a roasted nut shop in Toronto who wanted to know why we bought walnuts, pine nuts, and almonds every week. When we explained we were re-creating sweets from the 10th to 13th centuries, his eyes began to wander. Muna asked him, "Don't you think this is great? We're cooking in our 21st-century kitchen the desserts made in the kitchens of the caliphs and nobility one thousand years ago!" He looked directly at her and said, "If you told me what Madonna ate for breakfast, lunch, or dinner, well, that would pique my interest."

Most Syrians, instead, simply enjoy the food they are eating without brooding over its historical context. However, Syrian television has recently played a role in reviving the dishes of the past, especially by way of the *musalsalaat*, long-running television soap operas shown during the holy month of Ramadan, showcasing stories based on events that took place in Syria from the 18th to early 20th centuries. Scenes depicting family life feature dishes from that time. Thus, Syrians who watch these shows can relate to the same dishes that their grandparents and great-grandparents spoke about, prepared, and enjoyed.

Dishes such as hummus, baba ganoush, tabbouleh, falafel, shish kebab, and shawarma have reached international recognition. People tend to know these dishes as Lebanese food, but they are also Syrian, because the two countries were one nation until it was divided by Britain and France at the end of World War I. Yet these dishes from *bilaad al-shaam* survived—some as old as time; others created more recently to cater to local conditions and times. New vegetables such as tomatoes, potatoes, corn, and bell peppers, which originated in the Americas, made a huge impact on contemporary Syrian cuisine.

However, a lesser known niche of Syrian culinary history waits to be put on the world's tables, such as meatballs barbecued with cherries (*kabaab ma'a karaz*) (see p. 164), meat preserved in fat (*qawarma*) (see p. 62), the world's oldest cheese made into soup (*shawrabat al-kishk*) (see p. 97) or a toppings for savory pies (*fataayir bil-kishk*) (see p. 274), pomegranate molasses (*dibs rummaan*) used as a marinade for meat or dressing for salad, tangy sumac used to season food and prized by those with a low tolerance for salt, and the aromatic spice mahaleb used for centuries to seek God's blessings.

During the 19th and early 20th centuries, when Syrian food was virtually unknown abroad, it was a struggle for first-generation Syrian immigrants to express and preserve their culture by preparing their daily meals. However, it is now much easier for first, second, third, and fourth generations born abroad to obtain the main ingredients used in Syrian cooking, as they are readily available either in supermarkets or via the internet. For instance, prepared phyllo dough for baklava is readily available for only a few dollars. Grape leaves are packed in jars or sold loose in containers. The once sought-after dandelions that Syrians scrounged for in the open fields are now packed in bunches and sold in at many grocery stores. The triumvirate of traditional Syrian food—tahini, rose water, and pomegranate molasses—is not difficult to find. As for lentils, chickpeas, and bulgur, the health food industry now markets them as nutritious foods, something Arabs have known for centuries.

Over the millennial history of *bilaad al-shaam,* which has seen wars of foreign intervention, pillaging, civil and political strife, natural and unnatural disasters, along with centuries of intellectual movements and economic shift, trade and political exchanges—the people of what is now called the sovereign nation of Syria have maintained the social and culinary traditions that define them.

Our cookbook of traditional 18th- and 19th-century Syrian dishes has been a long time in the making. During this period of research and study, the catastrophic situation in Syria forced us to look at ourselves and our heritage, recognizing that a part of our history is being lost. A war against any country threatens not only the survival of its people but also, even more ominously, the destruction of social order, infrastructure, economic well-being, and security. The devastation of war has caused thousands to flee their homeland, hoping to return once stability has been restored. And as the droves of Syrian refugees have immigrated to countries around the world, they now face the challenge of settling in a foreign land with an unknown future. Their comfort zones are their language, music, dance, and food, which have become instrumental in bringing together new friends, neighbors, and colleagues to inspire a better and simple way of understanding Syria and the Syrians. The war in Syria that has caused so much destruction and devastation in that country has, in a way, boosted the food culture in other countries as Syrian refugees settle around the world. Syrian restaurants and cafés have mushroomed, and Syrian food appears increasingly at festivals.

Syria has suffered, yet the nation's story is one of survival and resurgence. The people of 18th- and 19th-century Syria under Ottoman occupation, and then British and French colonization and mandates, faced challenges, yet they did not give in. Their national identity, a major part of which was their food, represented the spirit of Syrians themselves: resilient, strong, and steadfast. Throughout the centuries of occupation and colonization, Syria has stood the test of time, with its people, whether inhabitants of Syria or refugees or immigrants, maintaining their identity—one part being their food. As the Syrian proverb goes: "A person's shirt does not change the color of their skin." Over the centuries, when life was unpredictable—as it is for many Syrians even today—the connection to their heritage stayed strong through their traditional dishes. The recipes not only gave life to those Syrians but also kept their homeland alive. Today, the Syrian kitchen, from village to town to city and beyond, continues to offer food that encapsulate the vibrant history of *bilaad al-shaam.*

On the homestead, circa 1930. Habeeb is second from the left. His mother, Shams, is in the middle.

From My Prairie Homestead to My Homeland

Habeeb Salloum

My quest to learn more about Syrian food is an outcome of my childhood on a prairie farm in Canada's province of Saskatchewan. I did not begin as a lover of Syrian cuisine, but rather, like other immigrants, I was overcome with an inferiority complex and believed the food my mother, Shams, cooked could not rival Canadian cuisine.

In the 1920s and 1930s, immigrants arriving in Canada from the Middle East wanted to be accepted, so they anglicized their names and did not teach their children Arabic. One reason for this may have been to give thanks for the opportunity to settle in this new land and begin their new life as part of Canadian society. Thus, they felt a need to fit into and emulate the dominant culture in whatever way they could. After all, Syrians had been subject to occupation and colonization that relegated them to second-class citizens in their own land. Now, as new Canadians, they hoped to be on equal ground. Ironically, however, the colonized had become the colonizer, the occupied the occupier, as Syrians, like other immigrants, settled on stolen Indigenous land. My parents were fortunate to have the opportunity to escape harsh conditions, yet our family reaped the benefits of our new life at the expense of others.

Day after day, as Mother cooked our delicious Syrian dishes, I coveted the bologna and sardine sandwiches that my school chums ate. Too ashamed to show them my food, I hid away in the back of the schoolyard and devoured my Arab bread filled with *labna* and fried zucchini. My food did not fit in.

My mother was a great cook. She grew up poor during World War I, when the Allied armies blockaded the Syrian coast and thousands died of starvation. I remember her telling me that in 1918, conquering British troops rested for the night in her village, and when they left the next morning, she and other young girls picked up the barley the horses had not eaten. They brought it home and ground it into flour to make bread. It was the only bread they would have for a long time.

As a young girl, she learned from these years of starvation and impoverishment, to improvise and to use what was available. Nothing went to waste. This was the way of life, the way to survive, in a land that had become void of sustenance, especially for the farmers and peasants of Ottoman-occupied Syria.

My parents brought these old-world traditions with them when they immigrated to Canada in the early 20th century. Ironically, they exchanged a harsh landscape of sun and sand and conflict for an even harsher one—drought, the Depression, tumbleweed, and Russian thistles. They settled on a homestead in southwest Saskatchewan, where they struggled through the great drought of the 1930s, to feed our family of ten with what they could grow in their own garden. But we never went hungry. We always had food on the table; and thanks to the old-country dishes my mother prepared, we were in good health. Mother made do with what she had, improvising with whatever cooking utensils and ingredients she had, substituting one vegetable for another; always laying a feast on the table, of the authentic and traditional Syrian dishes she learned to cook in her village. She prepared the same dishes for her growing family that she and my father were raised on. Besides providing us with nourishment, this was a way of maintaining our Syrian heritage.

When Dad left Syria, he brought a pocketful of chickpeas with him. The arid landscape and the hot sun of the drought-stricken Saskatchewan plains were conducive to growing chickpeas in our garden and it enabled Mother to prepare her nutritious dishes. The garden also yielded onions, garlic, fava beans, potatoes, zucchini, green beans, carrots, lentils, tomatoes, and cucumbers. Mother would use the wild herbs that grew around our prairie homestead (fresh or dry), and the few aging sheep and cattle we had were the foundation of the dishes she created.

Life back then was not as easy as it can be today. Working in the fields, lifting and digging, seeding and harvesting were backbreaking chores that we, as children, could barely tolerate. But the work had to be done. To survive, we needed to eat, so all of us pitched in.

Our daily chores included milking the cows. We drank this milk daily and sold the cream. However, my parents would make sure there was enough milk on hand so that Mother could make our weekly supply of yogurt.

Further, it seemed that mother could, on our little coal stove, make a meal out of any ingredient she found. For example, a type of *humayda* (sorrel) found on our homestead was an ideal substitute when she wanted to make stuffed grape leaves. *Dibs rummaan*, or pomegranate molasses, so important to Syrian meat dishes, was substituted with lemon juice. It didn't become available until after World War II, when more Syrians had immigrated to Canada and opened Middle Eastern stores, such as Abusamra Al-Khouri, a wholesaler-retailer in Montreal. When Mother stuffed zucchini or any type of summer squash, she used a corer that Dad had made and reserve the pulp for *'ijja*, a tasty Syrian omelet, for the following morning's breakfast. My father transferred his know-how from working the wheat fields of the Beqaa Valley to our prairie farm so that my family was never without bulgur, the staple grain Syrians cannot live without. The little wheat he was able to grow was in the sloughs, deep depressions in the land that retained a little moisture. Kibbeh, our family favorite, was made with it, and if we did not have meat during dire cold winters, a wild rabbit or chicken would suffice.

We cultivated our yearly supply of bulgur during the summer. We cooked the wheat, dried it out in the scorching sun, crushed it, and then stored it. During those early years on the homestead, we used the old-world method of removing the husks from the wheat: a mare pulled a stone boat round and round to crush the wheat, allowing the kernels to be removed from the chaff. It was my job to either sit on the stone boat or lead the mare for a couple of hours in a continuous circular motion until the job was done. This was also when we made *kishk* (see p. 59), the oldest cheese known to humankind. Our supply of *kishk* could last us the year.

My favorite time was the fall, when we butchered our sheep or steers. If the weather was cold, we put the meat in the shed to freeze. If it was still warm, we put some of the meat in pails and lowered them into the well—our form of refrigeration. The rest of the meat was cooked or made into *qawarma*—Syrian preserved meat (see p. 62)—and stored in jars. Even though we didn't have the traditional type of sheep tail fat used to make it, ordinary animal fat worked just as well. Animal hides were tanned, sheep skins were used to make mats, and Dad would make a crude form of footwear for us children from the cow or steer hides. No part of the animal was wasted. The feet, tongue, liver, kidneys, head—everything was cooked in different ways or made into sausages.

However, the highlight for me was what Mother made with the sheep stomach and intestines. She would clean them with soap and water over and over—perhaps dozens of times—stuff them with bulgur or rice (depending on availability), chickpeas, meat, and spices; and then boil them. Nothing tasted better. Years later, when the Royal Canadian Air Force sent me overseas, I tasted haggis in Great Britain and discovered that it couldn't hold a candle to the dish my mother made.

Fall also brings back the excitement of my first taste of ice cream. In the late 1930s, Dad surprised us with a used ice-cream machine. I still remember sitting with my mother and churning the machine handle for at least three to four hours. Made from 100 percent fresh cream, it is the best and creamiest ice cream I have ever had. It's possible that my partiality to vanilla soft serve today is a nostalgic reminder of our 1930s ice cream, or an homage to the first ice-cream cone served on this side of the world, which was by a Syrian named Ernest Hamwi, who used his *zalaabeeya* (fritter) as a cone at the St. Louis World's Fair in 1904.

Home-churned ice cream was a sporadic treat. Our everyday diet consisted of traditional Syrian dishes—kibbeh in numerous varieties, stuffed leaves, yogurt, *mujaddara* (lentil potage), chickpea stews and soups, and vegetarian or meat-filled savory pies. These were all enhanced with Mother's special touch with flavorings, seasonings, herbs, spices, and decorations, such as crushed dried chickpeas and homegrown oregano. When she needed tahini for hummus or sauce, Mother improvised with good old peanut butter; peanuts were also used for sweets, until walnuts became available. Rice pudding, probably one of the first dishes my grandmother taught my mother to make, was made during those early homestead years with bulgur, and since rose water and orange blossom water would not be available for decades, vanilla served as the flavoring.

Yet it is the baklava I remember most. In those days, when modern-age goodies were limited to Buck Rogers stories, it took Mother, with some help from us children, a full day of backbreaking work to make two large trays of this flaky, syrup-drenched sweet. Preparations to make the phyllo dough from scratch would begin very early in the morning. While the dough was resting, she would spread pristine white sheets over pillows, on top of a large table and sprinkle homemade cornstarch all over the sheets. She would then form the dough into balls, stretch each one over the pillow, and then gently, like an artist putting his final strokes on a masterpiece, pull the dough with her knuckles, until it was thinner than paper and near translucent. Quickly, she would cut the stretched dough to the size of the trays for assembling the baklava. Working fast, she lightly buttered each sheet as she placed it in a tray, until the trays were filled about halfway. Then she spread a delicious walnut stuffing over top and covered it with the remaining buttered sheets. She cut the baklava into squares or diamond-shapes and baked it until golden and crispy and then she spooned sugar syrup over it. The aroma was more than inviting, the taste superb.

Mother was proud of her excellent baklava, and other Arab Canadians who came to know her handiwork took pride in her accomplishment too. Even today, when I visit friends out west, I hear them say, "Shams used to make the best baklava in southern Saskatchewan."

Oddly, the rare times when we had a visitor on those barren plains, my mother would never serve them an authentic Syrian meal but would scurry around to find a chicken to butcher, and fry or roast it to make them a "Canadian" meal. Yet she always served the dishes with that special Syrian touch, thanks to her medley of spices and herbs.

Minot School, 1930s

My mother's dishes linked us to our homeland and kept us connected to our family back in Syria. Nostalgia—perhaps homesickness, for sure—could be alleviated by the taste of bulgur, kibbeh, or yogurt. To celebrate the good memories, we savored the foods that Mother had spent the day cooking. We would sit mesmerized, listening to our parents as they told the tales of the great metropolis of Damascus. I wanted to experience this world of wonder myself. Unfortunately, I didn't appreciate Mother's cooking until I left home. As the years went by and I traveled the Arab world, I realized that my mother really was a gifted cook.

My long culinary journey began back in the 1940s, during World War II, when I was in the Royal Canadian Air Force stationed in Montreal. During one of my leaves, I visited my aunt and her family in Pawtucket, Rhode Island. Aunt Raheeja, my mother's sister, prepared many excellent Syrian meals. Even though nothing tasted as good as my mother's cooking, my aunt's was almost as good.

One evening, my aunt presented a heavenly dish I had never seen before. When I asked its name, she replied, "It's called *kubba halabee*, patties made of ground lamb mixed with bulgur and spices. One of my friends from Aleppo introduced me to this recipe." She continued, "You know, the people of Aleppo make the best food in Syria."

This was my first introduction to the food of Aleppo. Over the ensuing years, I never forgot that dish—one of the 32 types of kibbeh for which Aleppo is renowned. Some twenty years later, I visited Aleppo for the first time and discovered that my aunt had been right. This city, considered to be the culinary mecca of the Middle East, has the best cuisine in the Arab world. That first visit kindled my love affair with the city. As a young man, I could only afford to dine in the people's eating places, where I was introduced to the true Aleppan kitchen. Among the numerous dishes I enjoyed, was an unforgettable dish called *kaftat halab* (Aleppo-style skewers of ground meat) in the modest restaurant Hagob, owned by a Syrian Armenian. Dining on bare wooden tables set over sawdust-covered floors, I relished every morsel of the spiced meat served with barbecued tomatoes. When I told the waiter how much I had enjoyed my meal, he smiled and said, "Should you travel the whole world, you will never find anything like the *kafta* of Aleppo, the best food ever created by human hands."

Habeeb Salloum, RCAF, mid-1940s

Over the years, I made a point to return to Syria every few years, now with my own family. We toured the country from north to south, east to west, visiting relatives and friends while experiencing the life of its people and traditions, many of which involved food.

On one such trip, we arrived in Aleppo and settled down in the Chahba Cham Palace, the most exclusive hotel in the city at the time. A friend had insisted that if my daughter and I were to truly know the joys of Syrian cuisine, we had to try the buffet offered on weekends at this hotel. That evening, I thought of his words as I surveyed the world of culinary splendor before us. For years I had been proud of my familiarity with Syrian food, but among the countless gourmet delicacies on the table were many that I was tasting for the first time.

Wherever Aleppans go, they take their dishes with them. In Toronto, we were invited to dinner by Leila Kronfol, a family friend who hails from Aleppo. Her mother, Hind, was visiting at the time and promised to prepare a real Aleppo meal for us. "It's authentic Aleppo food. I'm sure it will please you," she said as she ushered us to our seats. Soon we were enjoying *muhammara* (red pepper dip), *shawrabat 'adas ma'a al-silq* (lentil and

Swiss chard soup), *kafta mabrouma* (ground meat with pine nuts), and best of all, *kabaab bil-karaz* (barbecued meatballs with cherries). When I commented on how tasty the meatballs were, Hind replied, "It's much more delicious in Aleppo, where I use a special kind of bitter black cherry, only found around that city." *Nothing can be tastier than this dish,* I thought to myself—that is, until she set before us an amazing dessert called *ma'mouneeya,* a sweet semolina pudding, a specialty of her native city. It was a meal to remember—a fine reminder of Aleppo and its outstanding gourmet cuisine.

But let's not forget about Damascus. On one of my many visits to the city, I was invited to the beautiful Nadi al-Sharq, once one of the finest dining places offering the best of Damascene cuisine; from wholesome vegetable soups and stews, to richly flavored meat dishes, to sumptuous desserts accented with rose water and orange blossom water, such as baklava and *baraazik* cookies dotted with sesame seed and pistachios.

While meandering in the heart of the Old City, I came upon the Umayyad Palace Restaurant, where I enjoyed the choicest traditional dishes with a live band playing classical Arab music quietly in the background. What a spectacular setting it was, to taste the dishes of this city: *yabraq* (grape leaves stuffed with rice and lamb), *haraaq usba'u* (lentil potage, made even tastier with fresh pomegranate seeds), and the jewel in the crown, *ouzi* (a savory flaky pie stuffed with rice, meat, peas, and spices). My senses overwhelmed, I sat like a caliph of old, surrounded by the elegance of Arab culture in the first capital city of the Islamic Empire.

During my last visit to Damascus, in 2005, I learned from a close colleague about Abu Al-Ezz, a popular restaurant in the heart of the Old City that served the best of Damascene cuisine. Arab patrons and tourists alike frequent it in their search for authentic local flavor. Amid its traditional Damascene decor and music, the restaurant entranced us not only with its ambiance, but also with its dishes of grilled meats, stews, and much more, which allowed our taste buds to experience the best of what this ancient city has to offer. Today, many such great restaurants in Damascus remain operational despite the current conflict, anticipating that the war will end, and life will return to the stability that Syrian society once knew.

However, during our travels, it was in villages and towns where we enjoyed the most flavorful dishes, such as the lentil potage in Shahba, the spicy chickpea stew in Deir Atiyah, the stuffed intestines at the home of my relatives in Qaraoun, and the bulgur potage in Khabab. Perhaps it was because of my memories of Mother's cooking on the homestead, back in Saskatchewan, but it was more likely that these dishes expressed the true taste of my homeland and of my ancestors.

The traditional dishes of Aleppo and Damascus, and of the countryside between and beyond, are redolent of a world waiting to be discovered. Where once we ate our traditional Syrian dishes hidden away from the eyes of our non-Syrian neighbors, today's Syrian immigrants and refugees arriving at the borders of countries around the world bring their foods with them to enrich a more culturally aware and diverse public.

From left to right: Adeeb (Eddie), Habeeb's older brother;
Shams Salloum; and Habeeb Salloum

The Pomegranate Doesn't Fall Far from the Tree

Leila Salloum Elias
Muna Salloum

As third-generation Syrian Canadians, we have lived at the crossroad of two cultures all our lives. We are the descendants of immigrants who crossed the waters of the Atlantic to begin a new life in a new land without the comfort and security of everything they had lived and breathed all their lives. They arrived in Canada carrying their worldly possessions, knowing they would have to acclimatize to new surroundings. They did this with their know-how and their traditions.

Among these traditions from the old country were Sitty Shams and Sitty Nabeeha's Syrian recipes. One grandmother was an expert in the dishes of the villages and towns, and the other was proficient in the dishes of her native Damascus. These dishes, on which they raised their families during good times and bad, were the same foods that were passed down to them, and they continued to make them in their newly adopted country, where these recipes remained the most powerful link to their homeland. These traditional foods were a means of giving their children the tastes and aromas of Syria, with the understanding that these dishes were an integral part of their culture and upbringing.

We grew up knowing we had a rich and deep culture, and that Syrian food was a vital part of it. Our late mother, Fareeda, taught us the nuances of true Syrian food. For instance, when her homemade baklava came out of the oven, she would point to it and say, "This is Damascus, the aroma and the taste of my ancestors!" Sitty Nabeeha gave our mom her authentic family recipe for *safsouf,* a crunchy parsley salad her family enjoyed at least once a week in the ancient Bab Tuma district of Damascus. And Sitty Shams, our father's mother, taught Mom the dishes of rural Syria, such as *qawarma* and *kishk.*

Dad speaks highly of the creativity of Sitty Shams's meals and the way she was able to preserve the scent of the Qaraoun in faraway western Canada. We still remember visiting her and our grandfather Jiddy Jirjis as children and being welcomed with lots of kisses and hugs, and of course, a feast. After we ate, Sitty would sing old songs from her childhood, the same ones she sang to her own children, when memory served the purpose the internet does today. Sitty Nabeeha also sang the songs she remembered, in the hope that we would sing them as well. Language, song, and food evoked our grandmothers' memories of childhood, a time when they were happy, surrounded by family and friends, a time when they lived in Syria, no matter how dire the circumstances.

While Sitty Shams lived in the kitchen, Jiddy was busy in the garden. Whenever we went to visit them at their home in Swift Current, the city where they retired, Jiddy would almost immediately take us to his hand-watered garden and let us eat to our heart's content—the fresh green chickpeas and fava beans he had grown especially for us. He warned us not to eat too many to avoid an upset stomach, but those fresh pulses were like candy to us.

This was our world of food.

Everything tasted great. Sure, we enjoyed a hamburger here and there, but nothing compared to the kibbeh Mom made. She never used a food processor but rather a heavy manual meat grinder that churned out perfectly minced meat and onions. Mom would treat herself after all this hard work by feeding an onion through the grinder and wrapping it in fresh Arab bread. We couldn't fathom why she liked it so much. Freshly ground onion with a hint of kibbeh seasoning? Finally, we understood when we started making kibbeh ourselves. That wrap of Arab bread was an explosion of flavors, juices, and texture all in one bite, all from simple ingredients.

In middle school, we had our first introduction to certain cooking techniques in home economics class. When we learned to rub a garlic clove around the inside of a salad bowl and then toss it out, at home we got a lecture. First, Mom informed us, you never throw out food, and second, garlic is what makes food taste good. Our dad taught us that we should never throw away the water whenever we boil a pot of chickpeas or lentils, because it could be a delicious base for tomorrow's soup.

But our lessons went further. Mom wanted to make sure her daughters knew how to cook. After all, *"Tub al-jarra 'a timhaa, titlaa' il-bint la-imhaa!"* ("Turn the clay pot upside down, the girl turns out like her mother!"). In other words, like mother, like daughter.

Our first lesson: Arab coffee. Every Arab girl should know how to make it and how to serve it. Before the many Arab groceries and markets popped up all over Toronto, selling pulverized Arab coffee, we learned to start with green coffee beans. Mom taught us how to roast and then grind them to a near powder and then, with just the right amount of coffee, water, and cardamom, make the perfect cup of coffee. Most important was that third boil and removing just the right amount of *raghwa* (foam) to spoon into the bottom of each demitasse cup. Finally, pour the coffee into the cup slowly and carefully, because traditionally, the *raghwa* on top conveyed that the host had taken the time to prepare the perfect cup of coffee for the honored guest. Aromatic Arab coffee, with Umm Kulthum CDs playing in the background, reminds us of many weekend visits from family and friends. There is also the memory of Leila accidently spilling the entire pot of Arab coffee on the floor in front of her future in-laws, on her wedding day! The response? A chorus of *"Khayr, khayr"* ("Only good will come from this"), as a pot of spilled coffee is a sign of good luck and a blessing.

We eventually graduated from coffee-making to the art of rolling grape leaves to make *yabraq*. Now, this did not involve purchasing a jar of brine-soaked grape leaves. Rather, Dad would drive us to a park laden with grapevines—where poison ivy usually grew nearby. We would nip the leaves from their stems and toss them into big plastic bags. At home, Mom would take out her seemingly bottomless supply of clay containers into which we layered the leaves, salting them in between to preserve them. Later, the freezer became the means of storage. It took a few tries, but we both ended up being quite expert at rolling them, thanks to Mom's watchful eye.

As for the stuffing, the most difficult part was that Mom insisted we learn to cook Syrian foods the way she was taught—no measuring cups or spoons. Instead, we used good old sight, touch, smell, and most importantly, instinct. We knew there was enough rice, meat, or spices if the mixture looked right, felt right, and smelled right. We eventually got the stuffing down pat, with a few arguments here and there. However, most importantly for us, it was our special Mom and daughters time.

Alongside stuffed grape leaves came its essential accompaniment—yogurt. We were taught that no rice or bulgur dish is complete without *laban,* and we had to learn to make it. We stood dumbfounded for the entire lesson. After boiling the milk and removing it from the stove, Mom put her pinky into near-boiling milk and told us to count to ten, to see if her finger could handle the heat. Then it was ready for the next step. After she stirred in the *rawba* (yogurt starter), which was always on hand from the previous week's supply. Then Mom covered the pot and placed it in a warm place. And that was it. That was our lesson on how to make yogurt. No fancy implements, no measurements. No need to write anything down. We just needed to know how to count to ten. We thought Mom was joking around—until a few years later, when we attended a conference where an Arab American scholar was to receive a prestigious award in his field of study. After a five-minute standing ovation, he hushed the audience and explained that he was no different from any of us. After all, despite his two or three PhDs, he still made yogurt by putting his pinky in the hot milk and counting to ten. We took Mom seriously after that.

When it came to making meat and spinach pies, Mom would give one of us the job of making the dough, while the other was tasked with preparing the filling. The first time Muna pulled out a measuring cup for the flour, Mom laughed and explained that a sign of a good cook is the ability to use the eye to measure. As well, the feel of the dough determined whether it was ready to be filled.

Nothing could beat the aroma of savory pies baking in the oven, except for Mom's Arab and Canadian breads. Thursdays were delegated to the Canadian loaves and Fridays to Arab pocket bread or *marqouq,* large, round, paper-thin flatbread. Mom made the latter from rounds of dough that she would toss from hand to hand like a pizza maker, stretching it out thin and flat. *Marqouq* was our favorite, and Mom would always give us a crispy piece straight out of the oven to slather with butter. She would sprinkle the rest with water to soften, fold, and then store. For Mom's generation, and those before, bread was essential, and there was no choice but to learn how to make it. Although this was an all-day task, bread was necessary to complete a meal. You see, bread replaces cutlery and one cannot eat Syrian dishes without this "utensil."

But there were perks to this laborious process. Mom always put aside some of the dough—which was a sign of what was to come. Once the warm loaves had been piled high, as a thanks for our help, Mom stretched pieces of the reserved dough into elongated shapes and sizes, then deep-fried them. She called these a simplified form of *zalaabeeya* (see p. 304), and we ate them either sprinkled with sugar or dunked into honey. We later added a Canadian touch by dipping them in maple syrup.

We also remember her baklava. Like both our grandmothers, Mom made her phyllo dough from scratch. Even as little children we knew it was baklava day whenever we found her wedding rings sitting in a safe place on the kitchen counter. By the time we were ready for school, a large round cushion (*saj*) would be sitting in the middle of the kitchen table covered with a large sheet sprinkled generously with cornstarch. It was amazing to see a small ball of dough transform into two or three large trays of baklava in her hands. As the trays cooled, Mom constantly reminded us not to touch them. Yet, when Dad came home from work, those rules fell by the wayside. He had a tendency to nibble the top layer of at least one of the trays, much to Mom's chagrin. But she didn't really mind, because she knew that baklava was his favorite dessert.

Dad loved Mom's cooking, but he would sometimes remind her that his mom made something another way. He began to work in the kitchen, re-creating many of his mother's dishes. His favorites were anything with *kishk*, chickpeas, lentils, or *qawarma. Qawarma* was new to Mom, so Dad taught her how to prepare *mufarrika* and tabbouleh *ma'a qawarma*. Recipe origins aside, it was a general concensus that nothing was better than Syrian food.

There were also the little bits of wisdom that came with cooking and baking. Mom always warned us that if you drop a piece of bread, you should pick it up, kiss it, and touch your forehead with it. When we asked her why, she responded, "Because that's what I was taught. It's a gift from heaven." If you add the special spice, mahaleb, to the dough of certain breads or sweets, you are "spreading the *baraka*" (blessing). Other tips included adding an onion when boiling chicken to get rid of the *zankha* (any unpleasant taste or smell) and squeezing a few drops of lemon juice into the za'atar if it's not tangy enough. The best advice Mom left us with, is to cook with love.

Today, Leila's children know this is true. They roll up their sleeves to snack on *labna* (creamy yogurt cheese), *zaytoon* (olives), and za'atar. A bowl of *shawrabat 'adas* or *shawrabat hamra* is the kind of chicken soup that makes them feel better. And there is nothing better than knowing that their children are doing the same. A *labna* rollup or Arab bread dipped into a dish of za'atar takes precedence over Nutella or peanut butter. *Qamar al-deen* (sheets of dried apricot paste) are their preference over Fruit Roll-Ups, and *yabraq* and kibbeh satisfy any cravings for chicken nuggets or pizza.

Just as generations before, the traditions of our Syrian family will continue for generations to come as part of the legacy of our food culture. The recipes from the 18th and 19th centuries in this book reflect an older way of life, a time when those who had the means as well as those who did not used the ingredients that were available to them, through thick and thin, to feed the families of Greater Syria nutritious and tasty food. These dishes are a reminder of the past, of what was cooked in the kitchens of Aleppo, Damascus, and the countryside of *bilaad al-shaam. The Scent of Pomegranates and Rose Water* enables us to record the recipes of our grandparents and those who came before for posterity, before they become remote or forgotten memories. This book is an homage to our heritage.

Syrian Pantry Essentials

No kitchen is seriously Syrian without at least some of the following ingredients. Most are essential when preparing traditional dishes. The good news is that the 21st century has made these essentials accessible; most are now available at not only Arab and Mediterranean markets but also larger supermarkets. Yet despite the availability of these ingredients, many Syrians still firmly believe that za'atar from "back home" cannot be beat, or that the sumac from the old country is incomparable. Quite often, whenever someone is going to visit Syria, relatives place orders for them to bring back homemade *kishk* powder, *shankleesh* (cheese balls rolled in herbs or spices and aged), pomegranate molasses, and even home-brewed araq, the well-known Syrian anise-flavored alcoholic drink. Some say ingredients from back home are the best, whereas others believe they all taste just as good when they are prepared by loving Syrian hands.

Aleppo pepper *(fulful halabee):*
Aleppo pepper, also called Halaby pepper, is a spice named after the ancient northern Syrian city of Aleppo. It is a variety of *Capsicum annuum* whose pods are ripened to a burgundy color, partially dried, seeded, and then crushed or coarsely ground. Aleppo pepper gives the food a medium-spicy heat and a smoky, fruity flavor and is used especially in Syrian meat dishes. If Aleppo pepper cannot be found, replace with four parts sweet paprika and one part cayenne pepper.

Arab bread (khubz 'arabee):

Arab bread is usually defined as a soft, round, pocket bread often sold as pita—a Greek word borrowed from the Aramaic *pittaa*. It is ideal for sandwiches since it just has to be sliced in half and each side opened for fillings. A variation is *marqouq*, or *khubz al-marqouq*, a paper-thin, flat, foldable bread. It can be used as a wrap or rollup. Both breads are used as scooping spoons for any meal. Arab bread is widely available in Arab bakeries and stores, as well as many supermarkets, while *marqouq* is usually available in specialty stores.

Baharaat:

In Arabic, the word *baharaat* simply means "spices." *Baharaat*, or Syrian allspice, is a mixture of 7 spices (cardamom, cloves, coriander, cumin, nutmeg, paprika, ginger, and pepper) used in Greater Syria to pep up appetizers, pilafs, sauces, soups, stews, and all types of meat dishes. It can be purchased at Middle Eastern markets and specialty stores, sometimes under the name Seven Spices. However, we prefer to make the mixture fresh in small quantities as needed and store any leftovers in a tightly sealed jar in the refrigerator. To make *baharaat*, mix 2 tbsp allspice, 1 tbsp black pepper, 2 tsp ground cloves, 1 tsp ground nutmeg, 1 tsp ground cardamom, and 1½ tsp powdered ginger. *Baharaat* can keep for about three months, but it's a good idea to smell the spice blend before using to make sure it's still potent. If the aroma is very faint or nonexistent,

A Note about Garlic

In many recipes, such as soups, salads, and dips, we prefer to crush garlic with a mortar and pestle, or a garlic press, to create a smooth paste. Minced garlic is used for stews or other dishes when it's fried with onions.

discard it and make a fresh batch. The Indian spice mixture garam masala can be substituted.

Bulgur (Burghul):

Also known as bulgar or bulghur, this wheat product is made from kernels that are boiled, then dried and crushed. Bulgur has been used in the Middle East since the ancient civilization of Mesopotamia. It is famous today in Greater Syria and to a lesser extent in the surrounding lands as the main ingredient in kibbeh and tabbouleh.

Bulgur comes in three sizes: coarse (#3 or #4), medium (#2), and fine (#1). Coarse bulgur is used in potage dishes; medium and fine is used for salads, vegetarian and

Chickpeas

meat patties, and breakfast cereal.

In North America, cracked wheat is sometimes confused for bulgur. Cooked bulgur has a pleasant chewy texture, a nutty flavor, and a mouthwatering aroma while cooking—putting cracked wheat to shame. Also, bulgur resists insects, so it has a very long shelf life. When Habeeb,s family made bulgur on their farm, they could often store it for three years or more.

Cardamom (haal):

One of the world's most ancient and expensive spices, cardamom is an aromatic dried seedpod used to lend its unique flavor to coffee, tea, pastries, and other dishes. Arab coffee is not Arab coffee without cardamom! The seedpod has a thin, papery outer shell and contains small black seeds. Green cardamom is found from India to Malaysia, and black cardamom is found in parts of Asia and Australia. The type most frequently used in Middle Eastern cooking is green, which we have used for our recipes in this cookbook. Ground cardamom is more readily available and less expensive. Ten pods equal 1½ tsp ground. However, the seeds quickly lose their flavor when ground or exposed to air, so it is best to keep them in their pods until ready to use.

Chickpeas (hummus):

These legumes are known as chickpeas in English, *hummus* in Arabic, *garbanzos* in Spanish, *chiches* in French, and *cecci* in Italian. Chickpeas add a burst of mouthwatering flavor to simple dishes and make a pleasant change from pasta, potatoes, or rice. They can be prepared and served in numerous ways, with meat or without—in salads, soups, and stews.

Although it is more convenient to use canned, to harness the true essence of the chickpea, dried is the way to go. Soak chickpeas overnight in about 4 in (10 cm) of water, with about ⅛ tsp of baking soda per cup chickpeas, or ¼ tsp per pound. The baking soda will tenderize the chickpeas and cut the cooking time. Drain, rinse, and place them in a large saucepan. Cover with 4 in (10 cm) fresh cold water and bring to a boil. Cook on medium-low

Dried versus canned chickpea yields:

	Chickpeas	Yield
Dried	1 cup (200 g)	3 cups (500 g) cooked
Canned (drained)	15.5 oz (440 mL)	1 1/2 cups (250 g)
	19 oz (540 mL)	2 cups (330 g)
	30 oz (855 mL)	3 cups (500 g)

heat until tender, skimming off any foam. Drain before using. Boiled chickpeas will keep in the refrigerator for about three days.

Cumin (*kammoun*):

A small, slightly bitter fruit of the parsley family, cumin is dried and used as a spice in many Syrian dishes, especially those with chickpeas and lentils, and some meats and stews. A versatile spice, cumin adds a distinctive, earthy flavor to food. If stored too long, cumin loses its flavor and warm, agreeable aroma; hence, buy it in very small quantities. Alternatively, you can dry roast cumin seeds before blitzing them to a powder.

Fava beans (*foul*):

Known in Arabic as *foul,* these are also called fava beans, broad beans, horse beans, Windsor beans, or English beans in various parts of the English-speaking world. The mature fresh pods are large and green, containing several beans from about ¼ in (6 mm) to 1 in (2.5 cm) long. When favas are harvested very young, the entire pods—the beans and their shells—are tasty and pleasant to eat. These tender green pods make excellent snacks or hors d'oeuvres. Fava beans are more commonly harvested when they are mature, but still green. The seeds are then removed from the shells and served as snacks or used in a variety of cooked or raw preparations. Also, at this stage, the shelled beans can be frozen or canned. However, in most cases, the beans are allowed to dry on the plant before harvesting. Soak dried fava beans for twenty-four hours before cooking.

Freekeh (*fareeka*):

Also spelled farik and frikeh, this nutty ancient grain originated in Greater Syria and remains a popular staple throughout the Middle East and North Africa. Freekeh is green wheat that is harvested before it becomes ripe, giving it maximum nutritional value.

Fava beans

Before the advent of modern technology, it was spread out in the sun to dry. Then the wheat straws were carefully set under a controlled fire so that the straw burned but the seeds did not, because of the high moisture content remaining in the seeds. Originally, the roasted wheat was rubbed by hand to remove any chaff left on the kernels. This process of rubbing gave it the name *fareeka*—from the Arabic *faraka*, "to rub." The seeds were left in the sun to dry further, and then the kernels were coarsely ground.

Kishk:
This ancient powdered cheese made from two food staples—wheat and milk—contains most of the nourishment the human body needs. It is said the best *kishk* in Syria is made in the Qalamoun region. Fifty miles north of Damascus and fifty miles south of Homs lies the city of Yabroud, known for its high-quality wheat and goat's milk, both needed to make *kishk*. This, along with the long-standing experience of the city's *kishk* makers, whose traditional method has been passed down for generations, has given its *kishk* the top rank in the country. Usually, Middle Eastern stores will only have the fine grade. However, this near-perfect food can be made by following the recipe on p. 59.

Kousa:
Kousa is the Arabic name for a variety of small squash or zucchini. The type used in Syria are pale green, usually lightly striped, and bulbous at one end. Since these are occasionally hard to come by, recipes calling for *kousa* can use any type of small squash or zucchini.

Lentils ('adas):
This pulse comes in brown, green, gray, red, and yellow colors. Some types come split, which take half the time to cook. Middle Eastern cooks prefer the green variety. In the lands where lentils have been consumed for centuries, the number of soups and stews, dishes with meat and without, made from this pulse is legion. Lentils are flavorful and hearty with a meaty taste, so it's easy to believe that a hungry person, like the biblical

Lentils

Orange blossom water (*mazahar*):

Distilled water is infused with essential oil extracted from the fragrant blossoms of the bitter Seville orange, which is noted for its fresh citrus scent, more than its bitter fruit. Native to China, the bitter orange was introduced to the Iberian Peninsula by the Arabs in the 8th century and planted throughout southern Spain. Today, orange blossom water is a popular flavoring in Persian and Arab cooking. Just a few drops in cakes, candies, fruit salads, ice cream, puddings, pastries, stewed fruit, and syrups, brings the sweet perfume of the orange grove to the table. It is also used in countries such as Morocco and Algeria to rinse hair and hands.

Esau, who sold his birthright for a bowl of lentils, would give almost anything for a dish of this healthy legume. Red lentils cook faster than other lentils; thus, cooking times will change when using them in a recipe that calls for lentils. So, for recipes calling for red lentils, only use red lentils, no substitutions.

Mahaleb (*mahlab*):

This is an aromatic spice made from the pits of a wild sour cherry called *Prunus mahaleb,* which is used in certain breads, pastries, and cookies, such as *ma'moul bil-tamar* (see p. 295). It is available in Arab and Mediterranean food outlets as a powder or seeds. If necessary, substitute with ground fennel or ground cardamom.

Dry and powdered mahaleb

Chinese pine nuts are shorter and less expensive, whereas Mediterranean ones have a smoother flavor. Pine nuts are one of the costlier nuts, so in most recipes, slivered almonds, though not quite as tasty, can be substituted if necessary.

Pomegranate molasses (*dibs rummaan*):

In the Middle East, where pomegranates are much loved, the juice is reduced until it becomes a thick, caramel-like syrup that is used in everyday cooking, often as a replacement for lemon juice. It has a distinct sweet and sour flavor and is used to make drinks or to give soups and sauces a pleasing tartness. The taste of fried eggs or ground meat is always enhanced by a little pomegranate molasses.

Qawarma:

Traditionally in the Middle East, after animals were butchered, the fat was removed and melted. In case of sheep, fat from the tail was melted and reserved specifically for making *qawarma*. The meat was then cut into very small pieces and cooked in the fat with salt and pepper. Once the meat was completely cooked, it was placed with the fat in earthenware or glass jars, then stored in a cool place. With no refrigeration in the past, this was an ideal way to preserve the meat supply for the whole year. Today, instead of animal fat, some prefer to use vegetable oil or margarine because

Rose water and
orange blossom water

Pine nuts (*sanawbar*):

Also known as pignoli or piñon, pine nuts are white rice-shaped nuts taken from the cones of certain pine trees that grow on the shores of the Mediterranean Sea. About ½ in (1 cm) long, pine nuts have a smooth texture and a sweet, buttery flavor, which is at its best when the nuts are lightly toasted. They are also used as a garnish for rice and chicken dishes, and even for some desserts. For Syrians, they serve as the garnish for almost any dish. Store pine nuts in the refrigerator to prevent them from becoming rancid. Two varieties are sold in North America: Chinese and Mediterranean.

Saffron

they are more readily available. *Qawarma* is a main ingredient in stews, stuffed vegetables, and other dishes as a replacement for ground or cubed meat. To prepare *qawarma*, see p. 62.

Rose water (*maa' ward*):

Distilled rose water, made from the essence of red and pink rose petals, originated in the Middle East. In hot desert regions, fragrant rose varieties reach their apogee. The use of rose water in cooking was introduced to Europe by Crusaders returning from the Holy Land. In medieval Britain, the essence of rose became popular in drinks, jams, and sweets. Today, rose water is important in the preparation of Turkish delight and other sweets, as well as drinks. Use it very sparingly to add a mysterious, fragrant touch.

Saffron (*za'faraan*):

The deep orange dried stigmas of a purple crocus, native to the Mediterranean, are used to impart a distinct color, flavor, and aroma to cheese, eggs, ice cream, drinks, meat, pasta, sauces, soups, syrups, and sweets. Saffron is the world's most expensive food and can be purchased as a powder or in threads; however, threads are preferable—the powder is often adulterated. Before adding saffron to a dish, lightly toast a few threads, then crumble them in hot water. It is best to add saffron to a dish when it's almost done cooking, so as to preserve its color and flavor.

Sumac (*summaaq*):

These crushed dried berries, also spelled sumach or sumak, are used widely in Middle Eastern cuisine. This seasoning, with its lemony flavor, lends a tartness to meats, poultry, curries, fish, salads, sauces, stews, stuffing, and vegetables. In the eastern Arab countries and adjoining lands, it is also used extensively with onions and salt as a savory spice for roasts. Arab cooks are convinced there is no substitute for this tangy condiment.

Sumac

Za'atar

Tahini *(taheena)*:

Tahini, which is derived from the Arabic word *tahana* (to grind), is a tasty and nutritious sesame seed paste, with no cholesterol and very low sodium. It is somewhat like peanut butter in consistency and appearance but subtler in flavor. This delectable and nourishing thick paste, with a nutty taste, is the mayonnaise of the Middle East. Tahini is most closely associated with hummus, baba ganoush, and halvah (a flaky confection). It comes in two types: light and dark—the light version is considered to have both the best flavor and texture. In the Middle East, it's a long-standing belief that when combined with legumes, tahini becomes the ultimate edible.

Yogurt *(laban)*:

Known in Greater Syria as *laban*, yogurt is the universal sauce of the eastern Arabs, discovered some 5,000 years ago in the Mesopotamian plains. When made from skim milk, this near-perfect food is godsend for those wishing to reduce fat, cholesterol, or calories in their diets. Brands labeled low fat and low cholesterol can be substituted for mayonnaise or sour cream. Yogurt made from whole milk has a richer flavor and thicker texture and is still low in saturated fats and calories. When we make yogurt at home, we use whole milk for the best flavor. Besides being nutritious, yogurt is a marvelously versatile and adaptable food, adding richness, flavor, and an appetizing aroma to a myriad of dishes. It blends well with cheese, eggs, grains, meats, fruits, and vegetables, and makes an excellent marinade. Delicious when flavored with syrups, nuts, herbs, and spices, it enhances and is enhanced by other foods.

Za'atar (za'tar):

Originally an Arabic name given to various kinds of thyme and oregano, za'atar was used as much in 18th- and 19th-century Syria as it is today. Now the term "za'atar" refers to a mixture of various dried herbs and spices, including ground roasted chickpeas, marjoram, thyme or oregano, salt, and toasted sesame seeds, but sumac is always the main component. Each country in the Middle East, or even each city, town, or village boasts its own type of za'atar. As well, each family develops its own version of this tangy condiment. Its uses are many and varied—as a replacement for lemon or lime juice or vinegar; as a seasoning sprinkled on vegetables, salads, meatballs, kebabs, or *labna*; or as an unusually tangy dip mixed with olive oil and served with freshly baked bread. Nothing brings on the hunger pangs in the morning like the alluring aroma of *manaqeesh bil-za'tar* (see p. 281) baking in the oven.

The Basics

· · · · · · · · · · · · · · · ·

'Ajeenat al-Fataayir

Dough for Savory Pies

This basic dough recipe is designed for all types of savory pies, such as *fataayir bil-kishk* (see p. 274), *fataayir bil-labna ma'a qawarma* (see p. 276), and *fataayir bil-sabaanikh* (see p. 278). As the good ol' Syrian proverb goes: "In every village, there is a path that leads to the mill."

1 tbsp sugar

¼ cup (60 mL) lukewarm water

1¼-oz (7-g) package active dry yeast

3 cups (450 g) flour

½ tsp salt

⅛ tsp ground ginger

2 tbsp melted butter

¼ cup (60 mL) warm milk

½ cup (125 mL) lukewarm water

1 tbsp vegetable oil

Dissolve sugar in ¼ cup (60 mL) water, then sprinkle in yeast and stir. Cover and let sit in a warm place for 10 minutes or until yeast begins to froth.

Meanwhile, in a large mixing bowl combine flour, salt, and ginger. Then add the butter, milk, ½ cup (125 mL) water, and activated yeast. Knead well, adding a little more water if needed, until the dough becomes elastic. Do not allow dough to become sticky.

Shape dough into a ball, brush the entire exterior with oil, and place in a large bowl. Cover dough loosely with plastic wrap or a tea towel over top. Let sit in draft-free area and allow to rise for 2 hours or until dough doubles in size. Punch down dough, cover again, and let sit for 30 minutes.

Now it's ready for your favorite savory pie recipe!

Burghul Mufalfal

Basic Bulgur

Syrians have been eating bulgur for centuries. *Burghul mufalfal* was the dinner for villagers of the 18th and 19th centuries, and when travelers would stop for a night, they were offered the same dish along with bread and milk. It was a favorite across the region, so when Syrians began to immigrate in full force to North America in the late 19th century, they brought *burghul mufalfal* with them. A 1905 newspaper article describes "*nifelfel*" as a standard dish among New York's Syrian community. And in the Syrian grocery stores on Washington Street, bulgur was sold in "great bags." Syrians love their *burghul mufalfal* accompanied by yogurt.

4 tbsp butter (or olive oil)

1 cup (225 g) coarse (#3) bulgur

2¼ cups (530 mL) water

½ tsp salt

¼ tsp black pepper

In a frying pan on medium heat, melt butter, then stir-fry bulgur for 3 minutes. Stir in remaining ingredients and bring to a boil, then reduce heat to medium-low, cover, and cook for 20 minutes, stirring frequently to make sure bulgur doesn't stick to the bottom, adding a little more butter if needed. Remove from heat and stir, then cover and allow to steam for 30 minutes. Serve hot.

MAKES 4 SERVINGS

Ruzz Mufalfal

Plain Rice

In Syria, rice is always accompanied by a dish with sauce or broth, never eaten alone. Those who traveled throughout Syria and the Holy Land in the 18th and 19th centuries were quick to observe that *ruzz mufalfal* was always served with "sour milk." Centuries later, Syrians still enjoy the flavors and textures of yogurt with rice. It's timeless.

4 tbsp butter

1 cup (200 g) basmati or other long-grain white rice, rinsed

2 cups (500 mL) boiling water

½ tsp salt

In a frying pan on medium heat, melt butter and sauté rice for 1 minute, stirring continuously. Stir in water and salt, then bring to a boil. Reduce heat to medium-low, cover, and cook for 12 minutes. Remove from heat, stir, cover, and let sit for 20 minutes.

MAKES 4 TO 6 SERVINGS

Ruzz bi-Sha'eereeya

Rice with Vermicelli

Available in most Arab groceries, *sha'eereeya* is a thin vermicelli noodle that is used in soups and to add color and a buttery taste to otherwise plain *ruzz mufalfal* (see p. 54). Angel hair pasta, rice vermicelli, or spaghettini are perfect substitutes.

4 tbsp butter, divided
½ cup (70 g) *sha'eereeya* vermicelli
2 cups (400 g) basmati or other long-grain white rice, soaked in water for 20 minutes, then rinsed and drained

½ tsp salt diluted in 4 cups (1 L) boiling water
cinnamon for sprinkling (optional)

In a saucepan on medium heat, melt 3 tbsp butter and add *sha'eereeya*. Stir-fry for 2 minutes or until golden brown. Add rice and stir-fry for 3 minutes, then add salted water. Bring to a boil, reduce heat to low, cover, and cook for 15 minutes. Remove from heat, add remaining butter, cover, and let sit for 10 minutes. Transfer to a serving platter and sprinkle with cinnamon if desired.

MAKES 8 SERVINGS

Laban

Yogurt

The ancient yogis of India mixed yogurt with honey and called it the food of the gods. Cleopatra bathed in yogurt to give herself a clear, smooth complexion, and Genghis Khan fed it to his soldiers to give them courage. In Greater Syria in the 18th and 19th centuries, yogurt was a staple of life. And a 1902 *New York Times* column about the local Syrian community described *laban* as "similar to zoolak but thicker," zoolak being a type of fermented milk. Syrians everywhere cannot live without it. Rice and bulgur dishes and stuffed vegetables are placed on the dinner table with a side dish of yogurt, plain or as part of a cucumber salad. Traditional dishes such as *shish barak* (see p. 179), *shaakreeya* (see p. 120), and *makmour* (see p. 189) are accented by the signature yogurt sauce *labaneeya* (see p. 95).

Always set aside a few tablespoons of the yogurt as a starter for the next batch.

8 cups (2 L) milk

4 tbsp yogurt

In a pot bring milk to a boil, then reduce heat to medium-low and simmer for 3 minutes. Remove from heat and transfer to a bowl. Allow to cool to lukewarm temperature. (You will know that milk is cool enough if your finger can stand in the milk for a count of 10.) Stir in yogurt, cover, then wrap with a heavy towel and let stand for 8 hours. Refrigerate overnight before serving or using in food preparation.

MAKES 8 CUPS (2 L)

Labna

Creamy Yogurt Cheese

Labna can be purchased in Middle Eastern markets, but why not make it at home? This tangy, velvety cheese is one of the easiest to make because it is really just strained yogurt. No Arab breakfast is complete without a dish of *labna*. It is used in stuffing or is served on its own, complemented by a sprinkling of olive oil and mint, sumac, or za'atar. *Labna* is one of the first solid foods Syrian mothers give their babies.

¾ tsp salt

4 cups (1 L) yogurt

In a medium bowl, stir salt into yogurt. Pour yogurt into a fine white muslin or tight-knit cheesecloth bag and tie with a string. Suspend the bag over a bowl so that the water can drip out for two days, or until contents are firm. Remove *labna* from bag and place in a small bowl. Cover, refrigerate, and use as needed.

MAKES 1 CUP (285 G)

To strain the yogurt, Fareeda used a brand-new, white, tightly woven pillowcase that she would cut into "*labna* bags" and sew in a tie at the top. That was the way we knew how to make *labna*—that is, until muslin and cheesecloth bags became available.

Kishk

Powdered Cheese

Kishk

According to food historians, *kishk* is one of the oldest cheeses known to humankind. In the southern province of Hauran, *kishk* was one of the two most common dishes in the 18th century, especially in the winter. There were two types: one with leaven and the other with *laban*. During the 19th century, American missionaries traveling through the Syrian mountains noted that the people were poor, yet they were as healthy as the farmers of America. *Kishk* was the reason.

3 lb (1.5 kg) coarse (#3) bulgur

2 qt (2 L) yogurt

2 lb (900 g) *labna* (see p. 58)

1 tbsp salt

2 lb (900 g) *labna*, divided into 9 portions of 3 oz (100 g)

With a fine mesh strainer, rinse and drain bulgur, then let stand for 30 minutes. Mix bulgur with yogurt and let stand for 6 hours. Add 2 lb (900 g) *labna* and salt, combine well, and cover. Allow to ferment in a warm place for 9 days. Every day add 3-oz (100-g) portion of *labna* and stir.

After 9 days, roll mixture into walnut-size balls, then place on a white sheet in the sun to dry to a half-wet consistency. Depending on the heat of the sun, this should take up to three days. After drying halfway, separate balls from any dirt or debris that may have settled on the sheet and put them through a grinder twice on a fine setting, then return to sheet to dry in the sun. Rub between the palms of the hands occasionally to break up small clumps, then spread again by hand on sheet. Depending on the heat

Continues...

of the sun, it should take about three days for the *kishk* to dry completely. (Balls can be dried in the oven on very low heat, but the taste will be different.)

When the *kishk* is bone dry, pass it through a sieve for two types. The *kishk* that falls through the sieve is considered fine *kishk,* and that which remains in the sieve is coarse. *Kishk* does not need to be refrigerated, but it should be stored in sealed glass jars in a cool, dry place.

MAKES 4 LB (1.8 KG)

Qawarma

Preserved Meat

The traditional method of preparing *qawarma*, as described on p. 44, is a laborious process. Today, making *qawarma* in a modern kitchen is simple. In Syria, traditionalists still use animal fat. However, modern times breed modern methods, so *qawarma* is prepared with oil in many households. This recipe makes a minuscule amount compared to the quantity produced when *qawarma* was the cornerstone of Habeeb's daily menu.

2½ lb (1 kg) beef, mutton, or lamb fat (not suet), margarine, or vegetable oil (enough to cover the meat)

5 lb (2.25 kg) lean beef or mutton (any cut), diced into ¼-in (6-mm) cubes
5 tsp salt
2½ tsp black pepper

In a pot on medium heat, melt fat, then stir in meat, salt, and pepper. Cook, stirring occasionally with a wooden spoon to make sure meat does not stick to the bottom of the pot, for about 1½ hours. The meat is ready if it sticks to the wooden spoon when you lift it from the pot. Allow meat and fat to cool, then ladle into earthenware or glass jars, making sure meat is covered with ½ in (1 cm) fat. Discard excess fat.

There is no need to refrigerate *qawarma*. Once sealed in jars and stored in a cool place, *qawarma* should keep for at least a year.

If the *qawarma* was prepared with oil, place the amount of meat needed in a strainer to drain the excess oil. If the *qawarma* was cooked in fat, warm the amount needed on low heat, then remove meat with a slotted spoon.

Sals al-Thoum

Fluffy Garlic Sauce

There is no place in the world where garlic is enjoyed more, especially in sauces, than Syria. A neighbor once asked Mom if she could use garlic powder instead of garlic cloves in Mom's recipes. The answer? An old Syrian proverb: "*Mustarrakhas al-lahm, 'ind al-maraq tindam!*" ("If you use a cheap cut of meat, by the time you get to the gravy, you will regret it!") So always use the best ingredients for a better tasting dish. Smooth and light yet nice and garlicky, this sauce is a must-have accompaniment to any barbecued meats, especially chicken.

1 cup very fresh garlic cloves, peeled

2 tsp salt

4 cups (1 L) vegetable oil, divided

½ cup (125 mL) lemon juice, divided

a few drops of water

Slice each garlic clove in half lengthwise to remove any green center sprouts, as they impart a bitter flavor.

In a food processor, mix garlic and salt until finely minced. Stop a few times to scrape down the sides of the bowl.

While the food processor is running, slowly drizzle in ½ cup (125 mL) oil. After 3 minutes, stop to scrape the bowl, then restart the processor and slowly drizzle in 2 tsp lemon juice. After 2 minutes, stop, scrape the bowl, restart the processor, and add ½ cup (125 mL) oil. Continue alternating oil and lemon juice in slow, steady streams, stopping to scrape the bowl in between.

Continues...

When the oil and lemon juice have been incorporated with the garlic, add a few drops of water and process for 1 minute. The mixture should be fluffy and white.

Transfer garlic sauce to a container and cover with paper towel. (The paper towel removes some of the moisture, which would cause the sauce to separate.) Let sit at room temperature for 30 minutes. Cover with an airtight lid and refrigerate for 12 hours. Use as needed, making sure to refrigerate after use.

MAKES 3 CUPS (700 ML)

Taratour

Tahini Sauce

For Syrians, fish is lonely without this simple tahini-garlic sauce, the ultimate condiment. But Syrians also use *taratour* for other dishes, such as *lahm madda*, a type of *kafta* that is spread out in a pan, baked, covered with *taratour* when it comes out of the oven, and then baked for a few more minutes before serving. *Taratour* is a great dip for cooked potatoes or raw vegetables. Drizzle it over fried or grilled vegetables, such as cauliflower or eggplant.

4 garlic cloves, minced
¼ tsp salt
½ cup (125 mL) tahini

½ cup (125 mL) water
½ cup (125 mL) lemon juice

In a food processor, blend garlic, salt, and tahini. Add water, then lemon juice and continue processing until a smooth sauce forms. Place *taratour* in a covered container and refrigerate until needed. Use within 2 or 3 days.

MAKES 1 CUP (250 ML)

Qatr

Sugar Syrup

This is the traditional sugar syrup used throughout the Middle East in sweets and pastries, usually scented with rose water or orange blossom water, or sometimes both.

2 cups (400 g) sugar
1 cup (250 mL) water
2 tbsp lemon juice

2 tsp rose water or 3 tsp orange blossom water

In a saucepan, mix sugar and water and bring to a boil. Then reduce heat to medium and cook for 10 minutes, stirring occasionally. Stir in lemon juice and cook for 5 minutes. Remove from heat, then stir in rose water or orange blossom water. Let *qatr* cool to room temperature before using.

MAKES 2 CUPS (500 ML)

Mezza

. . . .

Dip into Kishk

During our many visits to Syria over the years, one of the biggest changes in food culture that we've observed is the younger generation's new love for fast food. The old way of making traditional foods, like *kishk*, from scratch has virtually disappeared in the big cities. Now, it seems, appreciation for this venerable food is limited to farmers in the villages of Syria and Lebanon and the descendants of peasant Arab immigrants.

1 cup (225 g) fine *kishk* (see p. 59)
¼ cup (60 mL) olive oil
1 large onion, finely chopped
2 small tomatoes, finely chopped
a few sprigs of parsley

In a small bowl, gradually stir cold water into *kishk* until mixture reaches the consistency of thick cream. Spread on a flat serving dish and drizzle with olive oil. Sprinkle with onion and tomato, garnish with parsley, and serve.

MAKES 6 TO 8 SERVINGS

Baaba Ghannouj

Baba Ganoush

Some believe the name for this dish, which means "spoiled daddy," came from the story of a woman who prepared softened eggplant to pamper her old and toothless father. Damascenes must have picked up on this tale, since this is one of the most loved dishes they eat to pamper themselves.

Eggplant

2 lb (900 g) large eggplant

2 garlic cloves, minced

1 tsp salt

½ tsp black pepper

¼ tsp cumin

¼ tsp coriander

4 tbsp lemon juice

4 tbsp tahini

4 tbsp olive oil

Garnish

½ cup (15 g) finely chopped
  parsley

½ cup (90 g) pomegranate seeds

¼ cup (35 g) pine nuts, toasted

1 tbsp olive oil for drizzling
  (optional)

Preheat oven to 350°F (180°C).

With a fork, pierce eggplant on all sides. In a baking pan, roast eggplant for 1½ hours, turning frequently until flesh is tender (a small knife can be inserted easily) and skin is crisp.

Allow eggplant to cool, then remove and discard skin. In a mixing bowl, mash pulp with a fork or potato masher. Do not use a blender or food processor, because that will render the pulp too fine. Set aside.

In a blender or food processor, place remaining ingredients except the garnishes, and blend for 1 minute, adding a little water if mixture is too thick. The ideal consistency is like heavy cream or corn syrup.

Add the blended ingredients to the bowl of mashed eggplant pulp and stir thoroughly. Spread evenly on a platter. Decorate with parsley, pomegranate, pine nuts, and a drizzle of oil (if desired).

MAKES 6 TO 8 SERVINGS

Kishkat al-Laban

Bulgur and Yogurt Dip

A simple, inexpensive dish, *kishkat al-laban* is popular in Damascus because of the two main ingredients—bulgur and yogurt—which are also the base of the powdered cheese *kishk* (see p. 59). This creamy, yet grainy dip was probably brought by country folk to the city, where it was spiced up to make an enticing appetizer.

½ cup (115 g) fine (#1) bulgur

1 cup (250 mL) yogurt

2 garlic cloves, crushed

1 tsp dried mint, crushed

4 tbsp finely chopped cucumber

½ tsp salt

¼ tsp black pepper

Garnish

2 tbsp finely chopped cilantro

2 tbsp walnut pieces (optional)

2 tbsp olive oil

In a bowl, soak bulgur in warm water for 10 minutes, then press water out through a fine mesh strainer. In a mixing bowl, combine all ingredients except the garnishes. Spread on a serving platter, cover loosely with plastic wrap, and chill for 1 hour. Decorate with cilantro and walnuts, and drizzle with olive oil just before serving.

MAKES 6 SERVINGS

Thoum

Damascus Garlic Dip

When the potato was introduced to Syria in the mid-19th century by the British Consul, the Damascenes made it their own. As for garlic, it was plentiful—so much so that in the 18th century, Egypt was importing it from Syria as the "grain of Damascus." If you like garlic, this twin of French aioli is addictive but simpler to prepare.

1 cup (325 g) mashed potatoes
6 garlic cloves, minced
¼ cup (60 mL) olive oil
¼ cup (60 mL) yogurt
¼ tsp salt
¼ tsp black pepper

Garnish
8 black olives, pitted and sliced
    in half
4 medium radishes, thinly sliced

In a food processor, blend all ingredients except olives and radishes until smooth. Spread on a platter, then decorate with olives and radishes. Chill, then serve.

MAKES 6 SERVINGS

Muhammara

Aleppo's Red Pepper Welcome Dip

This signature sweet and sour dish from Aleppo adds color to any mezza. Although it's not as well known as *hummus bi-taheena* (see p. 83), it is, in our view, a more inviting appetizer, with smooth roasted peppers and crunchy walnuts enhanced by tangy pomegranate molasses.

4 large red bell peppers

1½ cups (150 g) ground walnuts

1 tbsp *dibs rummaan* diluted in
    2 tbsp water

2 tbsp lemon juice

¾ tsp salt

½ tsp black pepper

½ tsp cumin

¼ tsp Aleppo pepper

4 tbsp pine nuts, toasted

2 tbsp olive oil

Preheat oven to 400°F (200°C).

On a baking sheet, roast peppers for 1 hour, turning a few times until blistered and brown on all sides. Remove from oven and let cool, then remove and discard skin and seeds. Place flesh in a strainer for 5 minutes to drain excess liquid, then chop very finely.

In a mixing bowl, combine chopped peppers and remaining ingredients except pine nuts and olive oil. Spread on a platter, cover loosely with plastic wrap, then chill for 1 hour. Just before serving, decorate with pine nuts and drizzle with olive oil, then serve with crackers or Arab bread. Make a day ahead and refrigerate overnight to enhance the flavors even more.

MAKES 8 SERVINGS

Hummus wa Rummaan

Tangy Pomegranate Hummus

With the profusion of chickpeas and pomegranates near Aleppo in the 18th and 19th centuries, it is little wonder that a dish with these two ingredients was created. This is a tangy variation on *hummus bi-taheena* (see p. 83).

1 19-oz (540-mL) can chickpeas, drained and rinsed

4 tbsp tahini

2 tbsp *dibs rummaan*

2 garlic cloves, minced

½ tsp salt

¼ tsp black pepper

2 tbsp olive oil for blending

2 tbsp finely chopped parsley

1 tbsp pomegranate seeds

2 tbsp olive oil for drizzling

In a blender or food processor, purée chickpeas, tahini, *dibs rummaan*, garlic, salt, pepper, and 2 tbsp oil until mixture reaches the consistency of peanut butter. Spread on a serving platter, then decorate with parsley and pomegranate seeds. Drizzle with remaining 2 tbsp oil just before serving.

MAKES 6 TO 8 SERVINGS

Hummus bi-Zayt

It's Chickpea Thyme!

The addictive chickpea, possibly one of Syria's oldest pulses, continued its popularity during the 18th and 19th centuries and was a specialty of Damascus. Simple chickpea dishes were sold as a quick, satisfying solution for the hungry stomach as people rushed around to get tasks done.

1 19-oz (540-mL) can chickpeas, drained and rinsed

½ cup (125 mL) olive oil

1 tsp thyme

1 tsp cumin

¾ tsp salt

½ tsp black pepper

In a saucepan, cover chickpeas with 1 inch (2.5 cm) water. Bring to a boil, reduce heat to medium, cover, and cook for 10 minutes. Drain and place in a mixing bowl. Stir in remaining ingredients. Crush chickpeas with a potato masher and serve immediately.

MAKES 4 SERVINGS

Hummus bi-Taheena

Chickpea Dip

Chickpeas

A 13th-century Arabic Egyptian cooking manual lists 10 varieties of this dish; one made with walnuts, almonds, pistachios, and hazelnuts, and spiced with cinnamon, caraway, coriander, and even salted lemons, was prevalent among those who could afford these ingredients. In contrast, *hummus bi-taheena* is an inexpensive yet full-bodied dish. To be Syrian is to have hummus as part of your daily diet.

2 cups (330 g) cooked (or canned) chickpeas
¼ cup (60 mL) water
4 tbsp tahini
4 tbsp lemon juice
2 garlic cloves, minced
¾ tsp salt
¼ tsp cumin

pinch of cayenne
2 tbsp olive oil for blending

Garnish
1 tbsp finely chopped parsley
2 tbsp finely chopped tomato
2 tbsp olive oil for drizzling

In a blender or food processor, combine chickpeas, water, tahini, lemon juice, garlic, salt, cumin, cayenne, and 2 tbsp oil into a thick paste. (If a thinner consistency is desired, add more water.) Spoon into a shallow platter and decorate with parsley and tomato, then drizzle with remaining 2 tbsp oil just before serving. Scoop up this thick dip with Arab bread or fresh vegetables.

MAKES 2 CUPS (500 ML)

Baleela

The Pulse of Damascus

The shouts of "*Baleela! Baleela!*" from street vendors in the souks and streets of Damascus selling steaming hot chickpeas guaranteed empty pots by the end of the day. This was a ready-to-go food, full of protein and, best of all, affordable. Today, it remains a common, hearty dish to start the day or a simple but nutritious appetizer or side dish. Syria's fancy restaurants elevate it with a topping of sizzling butter and toasted pine nuts. We enjoy it warm, especially on a cold winter day, but it's just as tasty cold.

In the past decade, *baleela* has made a strong comeback in Syria, thanks to the long-running popular television series *Bab Al-Hara*, which is shown during Ramadan. One of the main characters, *baleela*-seller Abu Ghalib, became a favorite among the viewers, who waited daily for his shouts of "*Baleela bi-l-baloukee*" in the streets of old Damascus.

2 19-oz (540-mL) cans chickpeas, undrained
5 garlic cloves, crushed
¼ cup (60 mL) lemon juice
¼ cup (60 mL) olive oil
½ tsp salt
½ tsp black pepper
¼ tsp cumin
3 tbsp finely chopped parsley (optional)

In a saucepan, bring chickpeas with their liquid to a boil. Reduce heat to low, cover, and cook for 15 minutes. While chickpeas are cooking, in a mixing bowl stir together remaining ingredients, except for cumin and parsley. Partially drain chickpeas, retaining ¼ cup (60 mL) liquid, and add to mixing bowl. Stir with a wooden spoon, crushing some chickpeas in the process. Sprinkle with cumin and garnish with parsley, if desired.

MAKES 6 TO 8 SERVINGS

Kubba Nayya

Syrian Tartare

No mezza is complete without a dish of *kubba nayya*, similar to steak tartare. Throughout Greater Syria, the meat is purchased fresh from the butcher the day it's to be eaten. Habeeb's mother, Shams, would use the old-country method of pounding the meat in a large mortar.

1½ cups (340 g) fine (#1) bulgur
2 lb (900 g) very fresh lean beef
    or leg of lamb
2 medium onions, puréed
1½ tsp salt
1 tsp black pepper
1 tsp cumin

1 tsp allspice
½ tsp cinnamon
pinch of cayenne
2 tsp dried mint, crushed
1 small bunch mint leaves
3 tbsp olive oil

Soak bulgur in warm water for 15 minutes, then press water out through a fine mesh strainer.

In a food processor, grind meat until smooth, then transfer to a mixing bowl. Add remaining ingredients except the mint leaves and olive oil and mix well by hand.

Spread on a platter and decorate with mint leaves. Sprinkle olive oil over top and serve immediately.

In some villages in Syria, onions sautéed in butter top each serving. Regardless, the best way to eat it is to scoop up a bite of *kubba nayya* with a fresh mint leaf and a piece of Arab bread.

MAKES 16 SERVINGS

Sujuq

Spicy Sausage Rolls

This delectable Aleppan dish of Armenian origin is sold all over the city, and its bold, spicy flavor is addictive. *Sujuq* is usually made with paper-thin bread, but we use an old family recipe for a buttery dough.

Aleppo pepper

Dough

2 tbsp water

1 egg, beaten

2 tsp vinegar

½ tsp salt

1¾ cups (260 g) flour

½ lb (250 g) cold butter

Filling

1 lb (500 g) ground lamb

4 garlic cloves, minced

1 tsp salt

1 tsp paprika

½ tsp coriander

½ tsp cumin

½ tsp ginger

½ tsp turmeric

½ tsp allspice

¼ tsp nutmeg

¼ tsp Aleppo pepper

4 tbsp olive oil, divided

For the dough: In a bowl, with a wooden spoon thoroughly mix water, egg, and vinegar, then set aside. In another bowl, combine salt and flour. With a pastry cutter or two knives, work butter into flour mixture until it resembles coarse crumbs. Tinkle wet ingredients into dry ingredients. Work dough until it holds together, but don't overwork it. Form into a ball, cover with plastic wrap, and refrigerate for 30 minutes.

For the filling: In a food processor, mix all ingredients except oil into a smooth paste. Set aside.

For the *sujuq:* Preheat oven to 350°F (180°C). Grease a baking tray. Roll dough into a square, less than ¼ in (6 mm) thick—the thinner the better. Spread filling over the whole surface of the dough. Roll tightly, then cut into slices 1–2 in (2.5–5 cm) wide and place on baking tray. Brush with 2 tbsp olive oil, then bake for 30 minutes. Remove from oven and brush with remaining oil. Serve warm.

MAKES 32 ROLLS

Kabid Miqlee

Fried Liver

In many parts of Greater Syria, calf or lamb liver is often served raw as a delicacy. However, this fried preparation puts all other liver dishes to shame. Serve hot and scoop up with Arab bread, making sure to soak up the juices.

4 tbsp olive oil

1 lb (500g) fresh beef, calf, or lamb liver, cut into ½-in (1-cm) cubes

4 garlic cloves, crushed

3 tbsp finely chopped cilantro or parsley

1 tsp salt

½ tsp black pepper

¼ tsp allspice

In a frying pan on medium, heat oil and sauté liver for 4 minutes on one side, then flip and cook for 3 minutes on the other side. Meanwhile, in a mixing bowl combine remaining ingredients thoroughly, then pour over liver and stir-fry for 2 minutes.

MAKES 4 SERVINGS

Lift

Pickled Turnips

This recipe is suitable for pickling many other vegetables, such as cauliflower florets, carrots, small peppers, green tomatoes, baby cucumbers, and string beans.

Damascenes in the 18th and 19th centuries loved their turnips, beets, eggplant, cucumbers, and, of course, olives pickled in fermented grape juice instead of vinegar. Turnips and red beets were available in the souks from early November until the end of March, and these could be pickled for future use. A dish of *mujaddara* (see p. 246) is always served with these colorful and crunchy pickled turnips.

4 medium beets

10–12 lb (4.5–5 kg) small white turnips, peeled and cut into quarters

6 garlic cloves, peeled

2 tbsp coarse pickling salt

10 cups (2.5 L) water

4 cups (1 L) white vinegar

Boil beets until tender, then peel and cut into quarters. Set aside.

Divide turnips evenly among 6 sterilized quart (L) Mason jars. Add 1 beet quarter, 1 garlic clove, and 1 tsp salt to each jar.

In a saucepan, bring water and vinegar to a boil, then reduce heat to low and simmer for 5 minutes.

Place a towel under jars and pour enough hot vinegar solution into each jar to cover the contents. Allow vinegar to settle, adding more if needed to completely cover turnips. Seal the jars, let cool, and store in a cool, dry place. Pickles should be ready in 2 to 3 weeks.

MAKES 6 1-QUART JARS

Makdous

Garlic and Spice Make Eggplant Nice

Mash *makdous* and scoop up each bite with Arab bread to savor their intense flavor.

When the *makdous* are finished, the leftover oil in the jar can be used to add flavor to salads or when sautéing onions and meat for soups and stews.

Makdous can last up to 1 year, in a cool, dark place or in the refrigerator.

When Habeeb was a boy, he had to eat these hidden away from his classmates' ridicule. Now he hides them away so that friends and family will leave some for him.

2 lb (900 g) small eggplants, about 3 to 4 in (8 to 10 cm) long, stems removed
1 head garlic cloves, minced
½ cup (50 g) coarsely ground walnuts
4 tbsp pomegranate seeds
½ cup (25 g) finely chopped cilantro
2 tsp salt
¼ tsp Aleppo pepper
olive oil

In a saucepan, cover eggplants with water and bring to a boil. Reduce heat to medium, cover, and cook for 10 minutes, or until soft (there should be a slight dent when pressed). Drain eggplants and allow to cool. With a wooden spoon, gently push down on each eggplant to remove excess water. Set aside.

In a bowl, mix remaining ingredients except oil, then set aside.

Make a slit lengthwise down the middle of each eggplant to form a pocket, but don't cut all the way through to the ends. Stuff with filling and gently close.

Place eggplants in a colander and weigh down. Drain overnight. Transfer eggplants to a large jar, cover with at least ¼ in (6 mm) oil, and seal. Let sit for 5 days, then serve. Make sure remaining eggplants are still covered with oil.

MAKES 10 TO 12 SERVINGS

Soups & Stews

Dried mint

Labaneeya

Yogurt Soup

Labaneeya is also the basis for the yogurt sauce in dishes like *shish barak* (see p. 179) and *kubba labaneeya* (see p. 173). You must have patience to prepare it, as the sauce must be stirred gently and continuously in one direction so that the yogurt doesn't curdle. For some Westerners this sauce is an acquired taste, but those who have the opportunity come to love it. When served as a soup, rice and bulgur dishes and any type of kibbeh usually accompany it. Enjoy hot with toasted and buttered Arab bread.

2 eggs, beaten	6 garlic cloves, crushed
3 cups (700 mL) yogurt	1½ tsp salt
3 cups (700 mL) cold water	2 tbsp dried mint
2 tbsp butter	

In a saucepan on medium heat, stir eggs, yogurt, and water until well blended. Stir gently and continuously in one direction until mixture comes to a boil. Reduce heat to very low.

In a frying pan on medium heat, melt butter, then add garlic, salt, and mint. Sauté until garlic turns golden brown, then stir garlic mixture into yogurt soup. Remove from heat and serve.

MAKES 6 SERVINGS

Shawrabat al-Kishk

Kishk Soup

One of the healthiest and most traditional soups, *kishk* soup is relatively unknown outside Syria and Lebanon. In the 18th century, residents of southern Syria's Hauran ate this dish for breakfast with bread, usually without meat. *Kishk* was at one time considered poor-man's or villager's food, but it has now become more common in Syria's cities, with dishes like *kishk* pies (see p. 274) and *kishkat al-laban* (see p. 76) being all-time favorites. Serve hot with toast.

2 tbsp butter

1 medium onion, finely chopped

2 garlic cloves, minced

¾ cup *kishk* (see p. 59), dissolved in ½ cup (125 mL) water

½ cup (75 g) *qawarma* (see p. 62) or very small pieces of fried meat (optional)

¾ tsp salt

½ tsp black pepper

5 cups (1.25 L) boiling water

In a saucepan on medium heat, melt butter and sauté onion until light brown. Add garlic, then stir-fry for 3 minutes. Stir in *kishk* and *qawarma* (if desired) and stir-fry for 2 minutes, then add remaining ingredients and bring to a boil. Reduce heat to low, cover, and simmer for 10 minutes, then serve.

MAKES 6 SERVINGS

Shawrabat 'Adas ma'a al-Silq

Lentil and Swiss Chard Soup

The two main ingredients of this rustic, nourishing soup appear in Arabic culinary texts dating back to the 10th century. The last two centuries of Ottoman occupation in Greater Syria were rough for the peasantry. Taxes had to be paid, and with little left to live on, soups, made with whatever was available, were the main meal of the day. Eaten with bread, they could satisfy a family's hunger, especially after a long hard day of work. Whatever wild herbs or greens were available would become part of the soup of the day. We've chosen Swiss chard because it's the most loved green for this type of lentil soup in Syria today.

1 cup (200 g) brown or green lentils, rinsed

8 cups (2 L) water

4 tbsp vegetable oil

2 medium onions, chopped

4 garlic cloves, minced

½ small jalapeño, seeded and finely chopped

½ cup (25 g) finely chopped cilantro

4 cups (144 g) chopped Swiss chard, leaves and stems

2 tsp salt

1 tsp black pepper

1 tsp cumin

5 tbsp lemon juice

In a saucepan, bring lentils and water to a boil. Reduce heat to medium, cover, and cook for 30 minutes.

Continues...

Meanwhile, in a frying pan on medium, heat oil and sauté onions for 8 minutes. Stir in garlic, jalapeño, and cilantro, then sauté for 5 minutes.

Add onion and garlic mixture to lentils, then stir in remaining ingredients except lemon juice, and bring to a boil. Reduce heat to medium, cover, and cook for 20 minutes. Stir in lemon juice and serve immediately. Try squeezing lemon juice over each serving to refresh the flavor.

MAKES 8 TO 10 SERVINGS

Shamaameet

Eggs in Mint Yogurt Soup

In 18th- and 19th-century Syria, the yogurt used to make *shamaameet* was more commonly made from goat or sheep's milk. However, in Saskatchewan, where Habeeb's family settled, Shams re-created the dish she grew up with using yogurt made from cow's milk. She would make *shamaameet* for her family often for breakfast or as a light lunch. It was a comforting dish on a cold winter day. Serve with plain rice (see p. 54).

4 garlic cloves, crushed
2 tbsp dried mint
½ tsp salt
2 tbsp butter

1 tbsp cornstarch diluted in 2 cups (500 mL) water
1 qt (1 L) yogurt
6 eggs

In a mixing bowl, combine garlic, mint, and salt. In a frying pan on medium heat, melt butter then sauté garlic mixture for 2 minutes and set aside.

In a heavy saucepan, combine cornstarch mixture with yogurt. Bring to a boil on medium heat, stirring continuously in one direction to prevent curdling.

Crack the eggs into boiling yogurt and cook for 2 minutes. Add sautéed garlic and mint. Cook, stirring continuously in one direction, for 15 minutes, then serve.

MAKES 4 SERVINGS

Shawrabat 'Adas ma'a Ruzz

Lentil and Rice Soup

On those cold, biting Saskatchewan winter days, Shams's lentil and rice soup would warm her family's chilly bodies.

5 tbsp olive oil

2 large onions, finely chopped

4 garlic cloves, minced

1 cup (200 g) split red lentils

1½ tsp salt

1 tsp cumin

½ tsp black pepper

½ tsp turmeric

⅛ tsp cayenne

7 cups (1.75 L) boiling water

¼ cup (50 g) basmati or other
     long-grain white rice, rinsed

3 tbsp lemon juice

4 tbsp finely chopped cilantro

In a saucepan on medium-low, heat oil then sauté onions for 10 minutes. Add garlic and sauté for 3 minutes. Add remaining ingredients except lemon juice and cilantro, turn up the heat to medium-high, then bring to a boil. Reduce heat to medium-low, cover, and cook for 40 minutes, or until lentils are tender. Remove from heat, then stir in lemon juice and sprinkle with cilantro. Serve immediately. Another option is to purée the soup in a blender (be careful when blending hot liquids), return to heat, and then add the lemon juice.

MAKES 8 TO 10 SERVINGS

Shawrabat Hummus ma'a Ruzz

Chickpea and Rice Soup

This was one of the popular soups in Shams's village, and she made it often when Habeeb was a boy.

- 4 tbsp olive oil
- 2 medium onions, finely chopped
- 4 garlic cloves, minced
- ½ small jalapeño, seeded and finely chopped
- 1 5.5-oz (156-mL) can tomato paste, diluted in ½ cup (125 mL) water
- 2 cups (330 g) cooked (or canned) chickpeas
- 1 tsp salt
- 1 tsp thyme
- 1 tsp black pepper
- 1 tsp cumin
- 8 cups (2 L) water
- ¾ cup (150 g) basmati or other long-grain white rice
- 4 tbsp finely chopped basil leaves

In a saucepan on medium-low, heat oil then sauté onions, garlic, and jalapeño for 10 minutes, stirring occasionally. Add remaining ingredients except basil leaves, then bring to a boil. Reduce heat to medium, cover, and cook for 30 minutes, then stir in basil and serve immediately.

MAKES 10 SERVINGS

Shawrabat al-Sha'eereeya

Vermicelli Soup

We enjoyed this pleasing combination of vermicelli and lamb in a friend's home in Damascus. After touring some sites south of the city on a chilly November day, we sat warming ourselves at the dining table with this quick dish. We have added some *dibs rummaan* for some tang.

2 tbsp butter

¼ lb (125 g) ground lamb

¼ lb (125 g) vermicelli, broken into 2-in (5-cm) pieces

1 tsp saffron threads, crushed

2 tsp *dibs rummaan*

1 tsp salt

½ tsp black pepper

⅛ tsp Aleppo pepper

5 cups (1.25 L) water

In a saucepan on medium heat, melt butter and sauté lamb for 5 minutes, or until it begins to brown. Add vermicelli and stir-fry for 3 minutes. Stir in remaining ingredients, bring to a boil, reduce heat to low, cover, and simmer for 20 minutes. Serve immediately.

MAKES 4 SERVINGS

Shawrabat Fajoum ma'a Lahm

Navy Bean and Lamb Soup

If navy beans aren't available, substitute any variety of small white bean.

The British Consul was credited with directing the first cultivation of the tomato in Syria in the early 19th century. Like other tomato-based dishes, this hearty soup of tender lamb and navy beans cooked with spices was most likely created in Syria in the mid-19th century. Serve this hot with Arab bread and pickles to offset the starchy beans.

4 tbsp olive oil

2 medium onions, finely chopped

4 garlic cloves, minced

1 lb (500 g) ground lamb

3 tbsp tomato paste diluted in 3 cups (700 mL) water

4 cups (1 L) chicken or beef stock

2 cups (330 g) cooked (or canned) navy beans

1 tsp *baharaat*

1 tsp salt

1 tsp black pepper

⅛ tsp Aleppo pepper

In a saucepan on medium, heat oil and sauté onion until soft, about 10 minutes. Add garlic and stir-fry for 1 minute. Add lamb and cook until browned, about 5 minutes. Stir in remaining ingredients and bring to a boil. Reduce heat to medium-low, cover, and simmer for 30 minutes, stirring occasionally, then serve.

MAKES 8 SERVINGS

Shawrabat Tarbiya

Creamy Meat Soup

Shawrabat tarbiya is a traditional Syrian soup from the time of the Ottoman occupation.

1 tbsp butter
½ lb (250 g) beef round or lamb, fat removed, cut into small pieces
4 garlic cloves, crushed
½ tsp salt
½ tsp white pepper
1 tsp *baharaat*
¼ tsp allspice
¼ tsp Aleppo pepper
6 cups (1.5 L) boiling water
1 cinnamon stick

2 bay leaves
4 tbsp butter (for roux)
4 tbsp flour
1 tsp salt
¼ tsp white pepper
1 cup (250 mL) heavy cream

Garnish

1 tsp paprika (optional)
¼ tsp Aleppo pepper (optional)
3 tbsp lemon juice

The Turks add egg yolks and lemon to their version of this soup. Some cooks use chicken, whereas others make it without chunks of meat but use meat or chicken stock. Vegetables like finely chopped onions, carrots, or celery can also be added.

In a saucepan on medium heat, melt 1 tbsp butter, then sauté meat until no longer pink. Add garlic, ½ tsp salt, ½ tsp white pepper, *baharaat*, allspice, and Aleppo pepper, and sauté for 5 minutes. Add water, cinnamon stick, and bay leaves, and bring to a boil. Reduce heat to medium-low, cover, and cook for 1 hour, or until meat is tender (if beef is used in this recipe, the cooking time will be longer). Discard cinnamon stick and bay leaves. Set saucepan aside.

In a deep saucepan on low heat, melt 4 tbsp butter, then stir in flour until bubbles form. Pour in meat and broth, 1 tsp salt and ¼ tsp white pepper, and bring to a boil, stirring constantly. Reduce heat to medium-low, cover, and cook for 10 minutes. Add cream, bring to a boil, reduce heat to low, cover, and cook for 15 minutes, stirring occasionally. Adjust seasoning to taste.

Transfer to bowls and garnish with paprika and Aleppo pepper, if desired. Serve piping hot with a squeeze of lemon.

MAKES 6 SERVINGS

Shawrabat Hamra

Syrian Chicken Noodle Soup

Tomato paste adds a hearty flavor to this traditional soup from Aleppo, Syria's contribution to the world's many varieties of chicken noodle soup.

1 lb (500 g) boneless skinless
    chicken breast

1 medium onion

2 tbsp tomato paste

2 oz (60 g) vermicelli, broken
    into 2-in (5-cm) pieces

1 tsp salt

1 tsp black pepper

⅛ tsp Aleppo pepper

3 cups (700 mL) water

3 tbsp lemon juice

In a saucepan, cover chicken and onion with water. Bring to a boil, reduce heat to medium, cover, then cook for 1 hour, or until chicken easily pulls apart with a fork. Remove chicken and set aside. Reserve broth and discard onion. Let chicken cool, then chop into ½-in (1-cm) pieces.

In a saucepan, stir remaining ingredients including chicken into 2 cups (500 mL) reserved broth. Add water and stir. Bring to a boil, reduce heat to medium, cover, and cook for 10 minutes.

Serve hot with a squeeze of lemon juice over each bowl.

MAKES 6 SERVINGS

Shawrabat Yakhnat al-Dajaaj

Hearty Chicken and Chickpea Soup

A soup perfect for a frigid winter day, *shawrabat yakhnat al-dajaaj* is medicine for Syrian immigrants who miss the sun amid the cold and snow of North American winters. In 1902, the *New York Times* commented that a "sort of pea, dried—'kummus'—that tastes like our peanuts ... gives a strong, rich flavor" to Syrian chicken soup. Wherever Syrians go, they take their love of the chickpea with them. *Shawrabat yakhnat al-dajaaj* can also be served as a stew over *ruzz bi-sha'eereeya* (see p. 55).

1 small onion, quartered

2 small cinnamon sticks

3 tbsp chicken broth powder

1½ tsp salt

1 tsp black pepper

1 tsp allspice

¼ tsp ground cinnamon

⅛ tsp Aleppo pepper

4 lb (1.8 kg) bone-in chicken breast, skin and fat removed, each breast cut in half

3 tbsp butter

3 tbsp olive oil

2 large onions, julienned

2 15.5-oz (440 mL) cans chickpeas, rinsed and drained

2 lemons (optional)

Continues...

In a large saucepan ¾ full of water, add quartered onions, cinnamon sticks, broth powder, salt, pepper, allspice, cinnamon, and Aleppo pepper and bring to a boil for 2 minutes. Add chicken and, if necessary, more water to cover, and bring to a boil. Skim foam and stir. Reduce heat to medium, partially cover, and cook for 1 hour, or until chicken can be pulled apart easily with a fork.

Remove chicken and place in a bowl. Strain saucepan contents into another large deep saucepan. There should be about 12 cups (3 L) of broth (if not, add a little water). Cover and keep warm on low heat.

Separate chicken from the bones and shred the meat—this should make about 6 cups (750 g)—then add it to the broth. Cover and cook on medium-low heat for 10 minutes, stirring occasionally.

While soup is cooking, in a large frying pan on medium heat, melt butter with oil. Add julienned onions and cook for 20 to 25 minutes, or until translucent and soft.

Add onions and chickpeas to broth and bring to a boil, then reduce heat to medium-low, cover, and cook for 20 minutes, stirring occasionally. Adjust seasoning. Then reduce heat to low, cover, and cook for 10 minutes.

Serve hot, with a squeeze of lemon over each portion, if desired.

MAKES 10 SERVINGS

Abou Bastee

The Father of Happiness

This dish is set on the table to cries of, "*Abou Bastee, kilou wa-inbustou!*" Eat and enjoy!

Abou Bastee is a centuries-old dish from Damascus. It is one of the few dishes that has retained its original form, because it tastes so good that nothing could be done to improve it. This stew brings happiness, delight, and joy to whoever eats it!

vegetable oil for deep-frying

1 lb (500 g) pumpkin, peeled and cubed

1½ tbsp butter

½ large onion, finely chopped

2 garlic cloves, minced

1 lb (500 g) lean lamb, cubed

¾ tsp salt

½ tsp black pepper

½ tsp *baharaat*

¼ tsp cinnamon

½ tsp coriander

⅛ tsp ground ginger

1 bay leaf

2 cardamom pods

1 small cinnamon stick

½ cup (80 g) cooked (or canned) chickpeas

1 medium very ripe tomato, peeled and finely chopped

2 tbsp tomato paste diluted in ½ cup (125 mL) water

½ tsp salt

2 tsp minced garlic

1 tsp dried mint, crushed

2 tbsp *dibs rummaan*

In a saucepan, deep-fry pumpkin in 2 in (5 cm) vegetable oil, then transfer to paper towel to drain.

In a large saucepan on low heat, melt butter. Increase heat to medium and sauté onion and 2 minced garlic cloves, until onions are translucent and begin to brown, 8 to 10 minutes, stirring occasionally.

Continues...

Add lamb, ¾ tsp salt, pepper, *baharaat,* cinnamon, coriander, and ginger, and stir for 3 minutes. Add bay leaf, cardamom, and cinnamon. Cover with 1½ in (4 cm) boiling water.

Bring to a boil, reduce heat to medium, cover, and cook for 45 to 50 minutes, or until meat is cooked, checking that water covers the meat. Meat is done when it breaks apart easily with a fork. Remove bay leaf, cardamom, and cinnamon.

Stir in chickpeas, bring to a boil, reduce heat to medium, cover, and cook for 5 minutes, stirring often.

Add tomatoes, diluted tomato paste, and ½ tsp salt. Bring to a boil, reduce heat to low, cover, and cook for 30 minutes, stirring occasionally.

Stir in pumpkin until just combined. Add remaining garlic, mint, and *dibs rummaan.* Adjust seasoning.

Cover and cook on medium-low heat for 15 minutes, stirring occasionally. Transfer to serving bowls with a garnish of fresh mint, if desired, and a side dish of *burghul mufalfal* (see p. 52).

MAKES 4 SERVINGS

Tabbaakh Rouhu

Syrian Soul Food

Once there was a king and queen who after many years of marriage finally welcomed a baby girl. The king named her Rouhuhu—his heart, his spirit, his soul. But the girl was a picky eater, so the king came up with a plan. Whoever could cook a dish good enough to tempt Rouhuhu would be rewarded with a lifetime position as royal cook. But finicky Rouhuhu refused them all. News of the contest reached a young man named Nader. When Nader presented his dish, Rouhuhu's parents were stunned to hear her say, "Mmmm, delicious!" When the king asked Nader the name of the dish, he could only tell the truth—that his mother had made it for him as a child and the dish had no name. At that, the king told the young man that he was the Cook of Rouhuhu (*Tabbaakh Rouhuhu*) to which Nader replied, "Then this is the name of my dish." This is best eaten with *ruzz mufalfal* (p. 54) or *burghul mufalfal* (p. 52).

There may well be a new name for this dish. While testing it for this cookbook, we doubled the recipe for our waiting guests, and as the paradisiacal aroma of mint and garlic permeated the air, one guest yelled, "Come on, this *tabbaakh rouhu* has *til'it rouhee* (stolen my soul). I cannot wait any longer to eat it!"

9 tbsp butter, divided

1 cup (175 g) zucchini or squash, cut into ½-in (1-cm) cubes

2 cups (500 g) eggplant, peeled and cut into ½-in (1-cm) cubes

2 large tomatoes, soaked in boiling water, then peeled and cut into ½-in (1-cm) cubes

1½ cups (225 g) finely chopped onion

½ lb (250 g) lamb shoulder, cut in small pieces

1 tsp salt

½ tsp black pepper

¼ tsp allspice

2 tbsp tomato paste diluted in 2½ cups (625 mL) boiling water

½ tsp *dibs rummaan*

1 tbsp dried mint, crushed

6 garlic cloves, crushed

1 lemon, cut in wedges (optional)

In a frying pan on medium heat, melt 2 tbsp butter and sauté zucchini or squash for 5 minutes. Remove and set aside.

In the same pan on medium heat, melt 2 tbsp butter and sauté eggplant for 5 minutes. Remove and set aside.

In the same pan on medium heat, melt 2 tbsp butter and sauté tomatoes for 5 minutes. Remove from heat.

In a saucepan on medium heat, melt 3 tbsp butter and cook onion, stirring, until soft, about 8 minutes. Add lamb, salt, pepper, and allspice, stirring well, and cook for 10 minutes. Stir in diluted tomato paste, bring to a boil, reduce heat to medium-low, cover, and cook for 20 minutes, or until liquid reduces by half, stirring often.

Add zucchini (or squash) and eggplant. Mix until just combined, then stir in tomatoes with their juice and *dibs rummaan*. Reduce heat to low, cover, and cook for 30 minutes, stirring gently occasionally.

Add the mint and garlic. Stir gently and cook on low for 10 minutes.

Serve the stew hot, with lemon squeezed over each portion, if desired.

MAKES 4 TO 6 SERVINGS

Sabaanikh ma'a Lahm

Spinach and Meat Stew

The 12th-century agriculturist Ibn al-'Awwam praised spinach as the "prince of leafy greens." The Arabs introduced spinach to Europe when they conquered Spain in the 8th century. Spinach was available in winter in 18th-century Damascus, so locals often prepared this stew. Have a dish of *ruzz mufalfal* (see p. 54) ready.

1 large loaf of Arab bread, split and cut into ¾-in (2-cm) pieces

4 tbsp butter

1 large onion, finely chopped

5 garlic cloves, finely chopped

1 lb (500 g) lean beef or lamb, cut into ¼-in (6-mm) cubes

3 tbsp finely chopped cilantro, or 1 tsp ground coriander

1 tsp cinnamon

¼ tsp allspice

⅛ tsp cayenne

¼ tsp ground ginger

2 tsp cumin

½ tsp black pepper

2 tsp salt

1¼ lb (570 g) spinach, washed and chopped into large pieces

¼ cup (60 mL) lemon juice

1 small onion, finely chopped, mixed with ½ cup (125 mL) white vinegar

There is a saying in Arabic: "*Is'al mujarrib wa laa tis'al hakeem*" ("It is better to ask one with experience, rather than one with knowledge"). Thus, it is best to go to the Arabs for their ideas on ways to cook spinach, thanks to their long history with it.

Preheat oven to 325°F (160°C).

Spread bread on a baking tray and bake for 10 minutes or until golden. Remove from oven and allow to cool. Place cooled bread in a serving bowl and set aside.

In a large saucepan on medium heat, melt butter. Add onions and garlic and sauté for 8 minutes or until onions begin to brown. Add meat, cilantro or coriander, all the spices, and salt and pepper, and sauté for 10 minutes or until the meat is browned. Cover with 1 in (2.5 cm) water, increase heat, and bring to a boil. Reduce heat to medium, cover, and cook until meat is tender, about 1 hour, stirring occasionally.

Add spinach and slowly stir until wilted. Cover and simmer for 5 minutes. Add lemon juice and simmer for 2 minutes. Remove from heat and pour stew into a serving bowl.

To serve: On each plate, place a portion of *ruzz mufalfal* (see p. 54), then spoon over a generous amount of stew. Sprinkle pieces of toasted Arab bread over the stew, then spoon about 1 tbsp of onion-vinegar mixture over the bread.

MAKES 8 SERVINGS

'Ayisha Khaanum

White Bean and Lamb Stew

'A'isha Khaanum was one of the wives of Naser al-Din Shah Qajar, ruler of Iran from 1848 to 1896, and she preferred beans over all other foods. So infatuated was she with beans, that her servants began to search for a special type of bean to make dishes befitting a queen. As luck would have it, a big caravan arrived carrying a bean uniquely tinged in a reddish color. The royal household's servants made the Damascene merchant's day by buying most of his bounty. The merchant set out for Syria, arriving there with the story of 'A'isha Khaanum and the bean dishes fit for a queen. As a result, the beans were a hit among Syrians, who still refer to them as *faasuuleeyaa 'Ayisha Khaanum*, the beans of 'A'isha Khaanum. Serve this over *ruzz mufalfal* (see p. 54), with sliced radishes and wedges of lemon.

1½ cups (300 g) white beans, soaked overnight in water mixed with ½ tsp baking soda

2 lb (900 g) bone-in lamb shoulder, cut into eight pieces

1 small onion

2 cinnamon sticks

4 cardamom pods

4 tbsp tomato paste diluted in 3 cups (700 mL) water

3 tbsp lemon juice

1 tsp salt

1 tsp black pepper

1 cup (50 g) finely chopped cilantro

⅛ tsp Aleppo pepper

In a saucepan, cover rinsed beans with 2 in (5 cm) water. Bring to a boil, reduce heat to medium, cover, and cook until tender, about 30 minutes. Remove from heat, let sit for 5 minutes, then rinse in cold water and drain well. Set aside.

In another saucepan, cover lamb, onion, cinnamon, and cardamom with 1 in (2.5 cm) water. Bring to a boil, remove froth, then lower heat to medium, cover, and cook for 1 hour, or until meat is tender.

Remove onion, cinnamon, and cardamom. Stir in remaining ingredients and bring to a boil. Reduce heat to medium-high, cover, and cook for 10 minutes, stirring occasionally. Stir in beans, bring to a boil, reduce heat to medium, cover, and cook for 15 minutes.

Serve immediately.

MAKES 8 SERVINGS

Shaakreeya

Yogurt and Meat Stew with Rice

Shaakreeya is labeled by many Syrians *sayyidat aklaat al-laban*——the lady of all yogurt dishes. Which is saying a lot, since Syrians really love their yogurt! The sauce can be served with any cooked grain, such as *burghul mufalfal* (see p. 52) or *ruzz mufalfal* (see p. 54) or *ruzz bi-sha'eereeya* (see p. 55), but the rice in this recipe has a richer, meaty taste.

In Damascus, people of all religions welcome the new year with a white dish for a fresh start. *Shaakreeya* is one of those dishes. Sometimes saffron is added to the yogurt sauce, as they do in the city of Homs, to give it a mellow yellow color.

Stew

1 lb (500 g) round steak, cut into
    1-in (2.5-cm) cubes

8 cups (2 L) water

1 tsp salt, divided

2 cups (500 mL) yogurt

1 egg, beaten

1 tbsp cornstarch diluted in ¼
    cup (60 mL) water

4 tbsp butter

1 medium onion, thinly sliced

4 garlic cloves, crushed

4 tbsp finely chopped cilantro

½ tsp black pepper

1¼ cups (310 mL) reserved meat
    broth

Rice

4 tbsp olive oil

1 medium onion, finely chopped

2 garlic cloves, minced

1 cup (200 g) basmati or other
    long-grain white rice

½ tsp salt

½ tsp black pepper

2½ cups (625 mL) reserved meat
    broth

For the stew: In a saucepan on low heat, combine meat, water, and ½ tsp salt. Cover and cook for 2 hours until the meat falls apart easily with a fork.

Remove meat and set aside, reserving 3¾ cups (935 mL) broth. If there isn't enough broth, add water.

In a food processor, thoroughly mix yogurt, egg, and cornstarch, then set aside.

In a saucepan on medium heat, melt butter and sauté onions for 8 minutes or until soft. Add garlic, cilantro, pepper, and remaining salt, then stir-fry for 1 minute and remove from heat. Let sit for 10 minutes, allowing mixture to cool somewhat.

Add yogurt mixture to the saucepan and bring to a boil on medium heat, stirring continuously in one direction to prevent curdling. Stir in meat and 1¼ cups (310 mL) reserved broth, reduce heat to low and simmer for 10 minutes. Remove from heat and cover to keep warm.

For the rice: In a frying pan on medium-low, heat oil and sauté onions for 8 minutes. Add garlic and sauté for 2 minutes, then add rice and sauté for 1 minute. Stir in remaining ingredients and the remaining reserved broth (2½ cups [625 mL]) and bring to a boil, then reduce heat to low, cover, and cook for 15 minutes, stirring occasionally to ensure rice doesn't stick. Add water if needed. Turn off heat and stir, then cover and let sit for 30 minutes.

Pile rice onto plates and spoon sauce over top.

MAKES 6 SERVINGS

Yakhnat Bataata ma'a Qawarma

Potato and *Qawarma* Stew

This combination of *qawarma* and stewed tomatoes creates a hearty, lightly spiced dish that is quick and very easy to make. Serve hot on its own or over *ruzz mufalfal* (p. 54). Either way, it's delicious!

2 tbsp butter

1 medium onion, finely chopped

4 garlic cloves, minced

6 medium potatoes, peeled, then diced into ½-in (1-cm) cubes

1 cup (150 g) *qawarma,* fat removed (see p. 62)

1½ tsp salt

½ tsp black pepper

½ tsp allspice

2 cups (500 g) stewed tomatoes, chopped

In a saucepan on medium heat, melt butter and sauté onion and garlic for 8 minutes or until they begin to turn golden. Add potatoes, *qawarma,* salt, pepper, and allspice, and reduce heat to low. Sauté for 5 minutes, stirring occasionally. Stir in tomatoes, then barely cover with water, and bring to a boil. Reduce heat to low, cover, and simmer for 25 minutes or until potatoes are cooked, adding more water if necessary and stirring occasionally.

MAKES 6 TO 8 SERVINGS

Cumin

Salads

· · · · · · · · · ·

Fattoush

Fried Bread and Fresh Vegetable Salad

During the Mount Lebanon civil war of 1860, a group of Christians escaped to Zahlé, where they were hosted by two families: the Fattoushes and the Skaafs. The refugees were welcomed to a table replete with tempting foods, but they did not touch the meat dishes because they were fasting for Lent. They especially enjoyed the fresh and crispy salad, scooping it up with bread. One of the Skaafs laughed and cried out to the Fattoush host, "Well, this is a new dish!" Then one of the Christians proclaimed, "From now on we will call this dish *fattoush*."

The bread used in *fattoush* can be toasted or deep-fried, but it should be added to the salad at the last minute—that is, unless you prefer soft bread.

4 cups (144 g) chopped Romaine lettuce

1 medium cucumber, about 6 in (15 cm) long, peeled and diced into ½-in (1-cm) cubes

2 medium tomatoes, chopped

1 medium onion, finely chopped

4 tbsp finely chopped cilantro

4 tbsp finely chopped parsley

2 tbsp finely chopped mint

2 garlic cloves, crushed

3 tbsp sumac (4–5 tbsp lemon juice may be substituted)

4 tbsp olive oil

1 tbsp lemon juice

1 tsp salt

½ tsp black pepper

2 cups (70 g) well-toasted Arab bread, broken into bite-sized pieces

In a serving dish, thoroughly combine all ingredients except bread. Then toss in bread and serve immediately.

MAKES 6 TO 8 SERVINGS

Tabboula

Tabbouleh: A Vegetarian Luxury

Tabbouleh spread from Greater Syria to other Arab countries and beyond, with Syrian immigrants bringing it to lands as far away as Brazil, where it is called *tipili*. True to the Arabic root of its name, which means "to season or spice," each ingredient lends its flavor to the others to create a zesty medley.

¼ cup (55 g) fine (#1) bulgur
2 large bunches parsley, finely chopped
1 cup (100 g) finely chopped green onions
½ cup (15 g) finely chopped mint

2 medium tomatoes, diced into ¼-in (6-mm) cubes
4 tbsp olive oil
4 tbsp lemon juice
1 tsp salt
½ tsp black pepper
lettuce leaves

Soak bulgur in cold water for 10 minutes, then press water out through a fine mesh strainer.

In a bowl, thoroughly mix bulgur, parsley, onions, mint, and tomatoes. Set aside. In a small bowl, combine oil, lemon juice, salt, and pepper to make a dressing, then pour over salad. Toss and serve on a bed of lettuce leaves.

MAKES 6 SERVINGS

The amount of bulgur used in tabbouleh varies from household to household, as does the amount of lemon and oil. And regional variations include other ingredients such as *dibs rummaan* and cucumber. What is standard, however, is that all vegetables must be fresh. The Syrian version often uses green onions.

Smeed

Bulgur and Fresh Vegetable Salad

Smeed may have all the familiar makings of its sister salad tabbouleh, but its base is bulgur instead of parsley. This was the villagers' answer to tabbouleh, a robust medley of tomatoey grain, fresh herbs, and vegetables hearty enough to be a refreshing one-dish meal.

Enjoy *smeed* by scooping it up with boiled cabbage leaves or freshly picked, tender grape leaves.

1 small can tomato paste

1 cup (225 g) coarse (#3 or #4) bulgur, rinsed and drained

1 large bunch parsley, washed, drained, and finely chopped

¼ cup (5 g) finely chopped mint

1 large tomato, finely chopped

2 small cucumbers, finely chopped

1 small sweet onion, finely chopped

1 small bunch green onions, finely chopped

1 large radish, finely chopped

¼ cup (60 mL) lemon juice

¼ cup (60 mL) olive oil

¾ tsp salt

½ tsp black pepper

In a salad bowl, rub tomato paste into bulgur with two hands. Refrigerate for 3 to 4 hours.

Mix parsley, mint, tomatoes, cucumber, sweet and green onions, and radish into the tomato-flavored bulgur. In a small bowl, whisk together lemon juice, oil, salt, and pepper. If you prefer *smeed* wetter, add another 2 tbsp of lemon juice and/or oil. Pour dressing over bulgur mixture and toss well. Refrigerate for 1 hour before serving so that the flavors meld.

MAKES 6 SERVINGS

Tabboula ma'a Qawarma

Tabbouleh with *Qawarma*

This version of tabbouleh with preserved meat and chickpeas is unique. Today, it is rarely prepared in the Middle East, except by those who keep the traditions of the past alive. It remains popular in the west Bekaa and Shouf regions, especially during the winter, when *qawarma* replaces the summer vegetables that are not available. We added parsley because it is available year round in North America.

½ cup (115 g) fine (#1) bulgur

½ cup (100 g) dried chickpeas, soaked overnight, then drained

3 cups (75 g) finely chopped parsley

1 small bunch green onions, finely chopped

¼ cup (5 g) finely chopped mint

2 medium tomatoes, finely chopped

1 cup (150 g) *qawarma*, fat removed (see p. 62)

1 tsp salt

½ tsp black pepper

2 tbsp olive oil

4 tbsp lemon juice

6 large cabbage leaves, cut in half

Soak bulgur in cold water for 10 minutes, then press water out through a fine mesh strainer. Place in a salad bowl and set aside.

While bulgur is soaking, wrap chickpeas in a clean cloth and with a rolling

Continues...

pin, break chickpeas in half, then pick out and discard skins. In a saucepan, cover chickpeas with water and bring to a boil. Reduce heat to medium and cook for 20 minutes, then remove from heat and allow to cool in their water. Remove chickpeas from water (reserve water) and add to bulgur, then stir in remaining ingredients except cabbage leaves.

Boil cabbage leaves in chickpea water for 3 minutes or until softened. Remove from water and place on top of salad. Serve immediately while the cabbage leaves are still steaming. Each person should be served one or two cabbage leaves with their portion of salad.

MAKES 6 TO 8 SERVINGS

Salatat Soureeya

Syrian Salad

We prefer Persian cucumbers for this salad, but other types will do as well.

Syrians like their salads light, colorful, and fresh, so ingredients are usually bought the same day they will be used.

4 medium tomatoes, cut into ½-in (1-cm) cubes

1 8-in (20-cm) long cucumber, or 4 small pickling cucumbers, peeled and diced

1 green bell pepper, seeded and chopped into small pieces

1 small sweet onion, finely chopped

½ cup (15 g) finely chopped parsley

4 tsp finely chopped mint

4 tbsp lemon juice

4 tbsp olive oil

¾ tsp salt

In a salad bowl, toss tomatoes, cucumber, bell pepper, onion, parsley, and mint. Just before serving, prepare the dressing by mixing remaining ingredients, then pour over salad and serve immediately.

MAKES 6 TO 8 SERVINGS

Safsouf
Chickpea and Bulgur Salad

Safsouf means "to mix things up." At one time it was made with only bulgur, green onions, mint, and eggs, because small isolated villages relied on what was grown in their gardens and what their chickens could provide. Today, almost everything is available and *safsouf* is made according to preference. Fresh tender grape, lettuce, or cabbage leaves are the "spoon" for this delicious salad. This recipe is Grandmother Nabeeha's.

½ cup (115 g) fine (#1) bulgur

4 tbsp olive oil

4 tbsp lemon juice

1 tsp salt

½ tsp black pepper

⅛ tsp cayenne

1 large bunch parsley, stemmed and finely chopped

1 cup (165 g) cooked (or canned) chickpeas

1 small bunch green onions, finely chopped

3 medium tomatoes, finely chopped

1 medium cucumber, about 6 in (15 cm) long, finely chopped

1½ cups (40 g) finely chopped mint

Make *safsouf* crunchier by substituting 1/2 cup (100 g) dried chickpeas for the cooked. Soak dried chickpeas overnight, then drain. A handful at a time, place chickpeas in a small cloth bag, or wrap in a clean tea towel, and break them up with a rolling pin. Remove loose skins before using.

Soak bulgur in warm water for 10 minutes, then press water out through a fine mesh strainer. In a small bowl, whisk together oil, lemon juice, salt, pepper, and cayenne to make the dressing, then set aside. In a salad bowl, combine remaining ingredients, then gently dress it. Chill for 1 hour, then serve.

Salatat al-Rummaan

A Salad with Crunch and Punch

The Syrians love their pomegranates, an ancient fruit grown for millennia in the rich northern plains. This light and refreshing salad is slightly tart yet tinged with sweetness. It pairs well with meat dishes as a palate cleanser.

1 cup (175 g) pomegranate
seeds

1 cup (175 g) cooked corn
kernels

2 cups (150 g) lettuce chopped
into bite-sized pieces

1 medium cucumber, about 6
in (15 cm) long, peeled and
diced into ½-in (1-cm) pieces

1 tsp salt

2 tbsp olive oil

2 tbsp white vinegar

2 garlic cloves, crushed

½ tsp dried mint, crushed

To remove pomegranate seeds, press and roll the pomegranate on a hard surface, then remove the stem. With a sharp knife, score the skin from top to bottom at 1-in (2.5-cm) intervals. Then the fruit can easily be broken into pieces with the fingers and the seeds removed.

In a salad bowl, mix pomegranate seeds, corn, lettuce, and cucumber. In a small bowl, mix remaining ingredients to make the dressing, then pour over salad. Toss and serve.

MAKES 4 SERVINGS

Salatat Burghul wa Jawz

A Nut and Grain: Aleppo's Domain

The Armenian community in Syria, the largest outside Armenia, has contributed much to the cuisine of northern Syria, especially Aleppo—including this dish. Syrians love their pomegranates, but the people of Aleppo love them the most. *Dibs rummaan* adds a tangy flavor to this salad's crunchy texture.

1 cup (225 g) fine (#1) bulgur

1 cup (100 g) finely ground walnuts

4 tbsp pine nuts

2 cups (50 g) finely chopped parsley

1 cup (100 g) finely chopped green onions

4 tbsp olive oil

2 tbsp *dibs rummaan* dissolved in 2 tbsp hot water

2 tbsp lemon juice

1 tsp salt

½ tsp black pepper

⅛ tsp Aleppo pepper

Soak bulgur in warm water for 10 minutes, then press water out through a fine mesh strainer. In a salad bowl, combine bulgur, walnuts, pine nuts, parsley, and green onions and set aside. In a small bowl, whisk together remaining ingredients to make the dressing, then pour over salad. Mix well, then serve.

MAKES 6 TO 8 SERVINGS

Salatat 'Adas

Lentil Salad

When Habeeb was growing up in Saskatchewan, none of his neighbors had ever heard of lentils, let alone tasted them. Yet his family thrived on them, since his parents had brought the pulse with them when they emigrated. Ironically, today Saskatchewan is the largest exporter of lentils in the world.

1 cup (200 g) green or brown lentils, washed

6 cups (1.5 L) water

5 tbsp olive oil

5 tbsp lemon juice

1 bunch green onions, finely chopped

2 large tomatoes, diced into ½-in (1-cm) cubes

1 cup (165 g) cooked (or canned) chickpeas

1 cup (25 g) finely chopped parsley

1 large red bell pepper, seeded and finely chopped

1 tsp salt

¾ tsp black pepper

In a saucepan, bring lentils and water to a boil. Reduce heat to medium, cover, and cook until tender, but still intact and slightly firm, about 20 minutes. Then drain and allow to cool, saving water for soup if desired. In a salad bowl, gently combine lentils with remaining ingredients. Serve immediately.

MAKES 8 TO 10 SERVINGS

Salatat Hindba

Dandelion Salad

While their neighbors were busy removing annoying dandelions from their land, Habeeb's family was busy collecting the tender leaves of the not-yet-flowering plants to use a side dish with onions, as a soup flavoring, or as a salad. As far back as the 10th century, Arab physicians prescribed dandelion greens for certain ailments, so a Syrian mother knows well what she is saying when she tells her children to eat their dandelions.

1 large bunch dandelion greens, stems removed, washed, drained, and chopped into bite-sized pieces

1 large Spanish onion, sliced very thin

2 tbsp finely chopped cilantro

4 tbsp olive oil

4 tbsp lemon juice

2 garlic cloves, crushed

1 tbsp sumac

½ tsp salt

½ tsp black pepper

1 large tomato, thinly sliced (optional)

In a salad bowl, toss dandelion, onion, and cilantro. Pour remaining ingredients, except tomato, over top, then toss again just before serving. Decorate with sliced tomatoes, if desired.

MAKES 6 SERVINGS

Khiyaar bil-Laban

Cucumber in Yogurt

As a child on his family's farm, Habeeb often enjoyed this cooling salad for lunch on a hot summer day, chilled in a pail hanging in the well—the Depression-era refrigerator. This was one of the first dishes Muna and Leila mastered under the guidance of their mother, Fareeda, as their grandmother Nabeeha nodded in pride.

2 cups (500 mL) yogurt

1 medium cucumber, about 6 in (15 cm) long, peeled and chopped into ¼-in (6-mm) pieces

2 tbsp finely chopped mint

2 garlic cloves, crushed

½ tsp salt

In a serving bowl, combine all ingredients thoroughly. Cover with plastic wrap and chill for 1 hour, then serve.

MAKES 4 TO 6 SERVINGS

Salatat Shankleesh

An Age-Old Cheese Salad

Syrians love *shankleesh* so much that no platter of mezza, glass of araq, or dish of eggs can do without this pungent, salty, yogurt-based cheese. According to many Syrians, the best *shankleesh* comes from their grandmother's kitchen, unless, of course, you happen to be in Tartus or Homs, the cities known for boasting about their cheese. *Shankleesh* requires a long and tedious process of manual labor to make, so it may just be easier to buy it from an Arab grocery, where it's sold as soft white balls with a mild taste or the older, darker, smaller balls, which have a more potent aroma and flavor. You will need lots of fresh Arab bread to scoop up every bite of this salad.

1 large ball *shankleesh*

½ medium onion, finely chopped

1 tomato, finely chopped

1 tsp za'atar

¼ cup (60 mL) olive oil

In a bowl, crumble up *shankleesh*, then mix in onion and tomato. Sprinkle za'atar over top and drizzle generously with olive oil. Transfer to a serving dish.

MAKES 6 SERVINGS

Salatat Shamandar

Creamy Beet and Tahini Salad

In the markets of 18th-century Aleppo, beets were available from November until the end of March. Their leaves were also used, at times as a wrapping for *yabraq* (see p. 185)

(see p. 185)

2 medium beets	½ tsp nutmeg
4 tbsp tahini	½ tsp salt
⅓ cup yogurt	½ tsp black pepper
2 garlic cloves, crushed	3 hard-boiled eggs, quartered

In a saucepan, cover beets in water and boil on medium heat until tender, about 1½ to 2 hours, then peel and finely dice. Place beets in a bowl and set aside. In a small bowl, thoroughly combine remaining ingredients except eggs, then gently stir into beets. Spread salad on a platter, then decorate with eggs and serve.

MAKES 6 SERVINGS

Coriander and *baharaat*

Meat

· · · · · · ·

Dul'a Mihshee
Stuffed Breast of Lamb

Habeeb's mother, Shams, would waste nothing. She would reserve the lamb broth to make soup another day. Refrigerate the broth overnight, then skim and discard the congealed fat. To 4 cups (1 L) broth, add 1 medium peeled potato diced into 1/2-in (1-cm) cubes, 1 large tomato finely chopped, 2 tbsp rice, 1/4 tsp salt, 1/4 tsp black pepper, 1 tsp dried mint, and 1/4 tsp cumin. Bring to a boil, cover, reduce heat to medium-low, and simmer for 40 minutes, stirring occasionally. Serve immediately.

Rich in flavor, with a medley of textures, *dul'a mihshee* is a specialty reserved for holidays, weddings, special occasions, and to honor guests in the most honorable of ways. Perhaps this is a legacy from times of tribal living, when Arabs received visitors, like members of their own family. A sheep was slaughtered, even if there was only one. In the 1879 novel, *Irene the Missionary*, John William De Forest describes the essence of a Syrian dinner in which, after an opening dish of "mejeddara," "a breast of lamb stuffed with chestnuts and raisins and supported by a huge pilaf of rice dotted with the yellow seeds of pine-tree nuts" is presented to the American guests. European and American writers in the 18th and 19th centuries often described Syrian feasts where they were welcomed with a *kharouf mihshee*, a whole roasted, stuffed lamb. Serve this with *salatat soureeya* (see p. 133) to cut through the fat.

Stuffing

4 tbsp butter
½ lb (250 g) lamb shoulder, cut into ½-in (1-cm) cubes
¾ tsp salt
½ tsp black pepper
¼ tsp allspice
¼ tsp cinnamon
1 cup (200 g) basmati or other long-grain white rice, rinsed
2 cups (500 mL) boiling water
2 tbsp pine nuts, toasted
2 tbsp slivered almonds, toasted

Continues...

Lamb

1 side of a breast of lamb, about 5–6 lb (2.2–2.7 kg) (ask your butcher for the right cut of meat), sliced to make a pocket between the skin and the rib meat	2 tsp salt 1 tsp black pepper ½ tsp allspice 1 whole medium onion 4 tbsp olive oil

For the stuffing: In a frying pan on medium heat, melt butter, then sauté cubed lamb until it begins to brown, about 8 minutes. Stir in salt, pepper, allspice, cinnamon, and rice. Add boiling water and bring to a boil. Reduce heat to low and cook for 10 minutes, stirring occasionally. Remove from heat. Stir in pine nuts and almonds. Set aside.

For the lamb: When stuffing has cooled, stuff the pocket in the breast of lamb and sew to close completely or truss with kitchen twine. In a large saucepan, cover stuffed breast with 1½ in (4 cm) water. Add salt, pepper, allspice, and onion. Bring to a boil, reduce heat to medium-low, cover, and cook for 2 hours.

Remove breast from its broth and let rest for 5 minutes.

Preheat oven to 400°F (200°C).

Brush olive oil all over lamb breast.then place on a baking tray. Bake uncovered for 20 minutes, turning once. Remove and let sit for 5 minutes, then serve immediately while piping hot.

MAKES 8 SERVINGS

Freeka ma'a Fakhd Ghanam

Leg of Lamb with Freekeh

European Orientalist travelers to Greater Syria in the late 18th and early 19th centuries wrote of the Syrians eating "ferik," unripe ears of wheat baked in an oven and then boiled with meat, a method practiced by their ancestors.

In 2300 BCE, a Syrian village, anticipating an attack that would result in the loss of their wheat crops, picked the early green heads of the wheat and stored them. The enemy arrived and set fire to the stockpiled wheat and left after devastating the area. However, the people of the village discovered that when they rubbed away the burned chaff, they found roasted wheat kernels inside. Thus, the Arabic word *farika*, meaning "to rub," was used to name this green grain.

4–5 lb (1.8–2.2 kg) leg of lamb
10 cups (2.5 L) water
bouquet garni—a tied cheese-cloth bag containing 10 cardamom pods, 6 peppercorns, 1 medium onion, 4 garlic cloves, 4 3-in (8-cm) cinnamon sticks, 6 cloves, and 4 bay leaves

1½ tsp salt, divided
1 tsp black pepper
¼ tsp Aleppo pepper
¾ cup (175 mL) yogurt
1½ cups (340 g) freekeh, thoroughly washed and drained
2 tbsp pine nuts, toasted

Preheat oven to 400°F (200°C).

In a roasting pan on the stovetop on medium-high heat, bring lamb and water to a boil, skimming to remove froth. Remove from heat, add bouquet

Continues...

garni, cover, and roast in the oven for 2 hours, or until meat pulls apart easily with a fork.

Place lamb in another roasting pan, reserving 3½ cups (830 mL) of lamb stock. Sprinkle on all sides with 1 tsp salt, black pepper, and Aleppo pepper. When lamb has slightly cooled, rub entire leg with yogurt. Return to oven and roast for 15 minutes, turning once. Set aside and keep warm.

In a saucepan, bring freekeh, ½ tsp salt, and reserved stock to a boil. Reduce heat to medium-low, cover, and simmer for 15 minutes, or until freekeh is soft and all liquid has been absorbed. Remove from heat, stir, and cover, then let stand for 20 minutes.

Spread freekeh on a serving platter and place the leg of lamb on top. Decorate with pine nuts and serve with yogurt.

MAKES 6 SERVINGS

Baamiya bil-Mawzaat

Lamb Shanks with Okra

Originally from Africa, okra appeared in the palaces of the Ottomans in the late 17th century. By early 19th century, it had become one of the new ingredients in the Syrian kitchen, and by the end of the century it was vastly cultivated in the country. It remains a popular vegetable in Syria, Lebanon, Palestine, and Iraq. Serve this hearty stew immediately, spooned over *ruzz mufalfal* (see p. 54) with *makdous* (see p. 91) on the side.

Pomegranate molasses

2½ lb (1 kg) lamb shanks, trimmed of excess fat

4 bay leaves

1 lb (500 g) fresh okra, or frozen and thawed

vegetable oil for deep-frying

4 tbsp butter

1 medium onion, finely chopped

1½ tsp salt

1 tsp black pepper

1 lb (500 g) tomatoes, finely chopped

2 tbsp tomato paste

2 tbsp *dibs rummaan,* or 2 tbsp lemon juice

8 garlic cloves, crushed

2 cups (100 g) chopped cilantro

In a saucepan, cover lamb and bay leaves with 2 in (5 cm) water. Bring to a boil, skimming to remove froth. Reduce heat to medium, cover, and cook for

1½ hours or until meat can be easily pulled off the bone. Remove shanks and set aside. Discard bay leaves, but reserve broth.

While the shanks are cooking, deep-fry okra whole in oil for 5 minutes or until they begin to brown, then drain on paper towel.

In a saucepan on medium heat, melt butter and sauté onion for 8 minutes. Add salt and pepper and cook for 2 minutes. Add tomatoes, tomato paste, and 2 cups (500 mL) broth, cover, and cook for 5 minutes. Add shanks, cover and cook for 10 minutes, stirring occasionally. Add *dibs rumaan* and mix well. Reduce heat to low and simmer for 2 minutes. Gently stir in okra and cook for 5 minutes, stirring occasionally. Stir in garlic and cilantro and cook for 2 minutes. Serve immediately.

MAKES 4 SERVINGS

Okra is delicious cooked with tomatoes in oil and served as a side dish or cooked with meat, as in this recipe. At one time, lamb shanks were a popular meat for various stews in Syria but have now been replaced with cubes of meat for easier dining.

Jidee bil-Zayt

Lamb Shanks in Oil

In his 10th-century cooking manual, Ibn Sayyar al-Warraq lauds goat meat (*lahm al-jidee*) as being perfect for balancing the body humors. Good advice lasts a lifetime, or in this case, centuries. But since goat meat is not always readily available, we opted for lamb shanks, which, we must admit, turned out just as tasty. We love any combination of garlic and lamb.

10 garlic cloves, divided

1½ tsp salt, divided

¼ tsp black pepper

½ tsp *baharaat*

½ tsp coriander

⅛ tsp cinnamon

pinch cayenne

⅛ tsp ground ginger

2 tbsp lemon juice

1½ tbsp olive oil

2 tbsp melted butter

2 lamb shanks, trimmed of
    excess fat and scored

¼ cup (60 mL) + 2½ tbsp olive oil

1 bay leaf

2 cardamom pods

1 cinnamon stick

1 cup (50 g) finely chopped
    cilantro

2 cups (650 g) 1-in (2.5-cm)
    potato cubes, deep-fried

1 lemon, cut into wedges

Crush 4 garlic cloves. In a small bowl, combine garlic, ¾ tsp salt, pepper, *baharaat*, coriander, cinnamon, cayenne, ginger, lemon juice, 1½ tbsp oil, and butter. Rub all over and into shanks.

In a large saucepan on medium-high, heat ¼ cup (60 mL) oil and brown shanks, turning for an even color, about 10 minutes. Add boiling water to cover 1 in (2.5 cm), then add remaining salt, bay leaf, cardamom, and cinnamon stick. Reduce heat to medium-low, cover, and cook for 1 hour and 20 minutes, or until meat is tender and falling off the bone. Remove shanks and keep warm. Strain and reserve 1 cup (250 mL) broth.

While meat is cooking, crush remaining garlic cloves. In a frying pan on medium high, heat 1 tbsp oil and sauté garlic for 1 minute, then add cilantro and sauté for 3 minutes. Remove from heat.

Return meat to saucepan and gently stir in potatoes. Stir in cilantro-garlic mixture, then add ½ cup (125 mL) reserved broth. Adjust seasoning. Bring to a boil, reduce heat to low, cover, and cook for 15 minutes.

Arrange shanks on a serving platter with potatoes and cilantro-garlic and top with lemon wedges for each person to squeeze over their portion. Serve immediately with remaining broth in a bowl on the side.

MAKES 2 SERVINGS

Kirsh Mihshee

Stuffed Sheep Stomach

On the farm, Habeeb always looked forward to autumn. That's when his father would butcher a few sheep or a steer for the family's winter supply of meat. Habeeb's mouth used to water in anticipation of the annual feast of stuffed stomach. As she had done many times in Syria, his mother would spend hours cleaning the sheep and steer stomach and intestines, first scrubbing the outside with soap, then turning them inside out to repeat the procedure. She would do this several times, then soak the clean organs in salt and vinegar, and store them in the cold shed ready to be stuffed the next day. Today, life is easier; butcher shops or meat counters can clean the stomach for you.

It is said that one of the favorite dishes of the 7th-century Umayyad caliph Muawiya was stuffed stomach. Syrians have continued the tradition ever since.

1 sheep stomach, scraped, then scrubbed with soap and washed thoroughly

6 tsp salt, divided

4 tbsp white vinegar

1 tsp allspice

1 tsp garlic powder

4 tbsp butter

½ lb (250 g) lamb shoulder, cut into ½-in (1-cm) cubes

4 large onions, finely chopped

2 cups (330 g) split or full cooked (or canned) chickpeas

1½ cups (300 g) basmati or other long-grain white rice

1 tsp black pepper

½ tsp nutmeg

½ tsp cinnamon

4 tbsp pine nuts, toasted

Cut stomach into 4 pieces then rub each piece with 1 tsp of salt. In a bowl, cover pieces with water and add vinegar. Let stand overnight, then drain and thoroughly wash, then dry.

Combine allspice and garlic powder, then rub both inside and outside of the stomach pieces. Sew each piece along three sides to form a bag.

For the stuffing: In a frying pan on medium heat, melt butter then sauté lamb for 5 minutes, until it begins to brown. Stir in remaining 2 tsp salt, three-quarters of the onions, and remaining ingredients, then set aside.

Stuff stomach bags, then sew the openings shut. In a large saucepan, cover stuffed stomach and remaining onions with 3 in (8 cm) of water and bring to a boil. Cook on medium heat for 1 hour and 15 minutes, adding more water to cover if necessary.

Serve stuffed stomach hot with broth, after seasoning to taste with salt, pepper, and cumin.

MAKES 6 SERVINGS

Daawoud Baasha

Meatballs in Tomato Sauce

According to legend, this dish is named after Daawoud Baasha, an Ottoman pasha who governed Mount Lebanon in the late 18th century. He loved the dish so much, he had it prepared daily. Serve this hot with *ruzz mufalfal* (see p. 54) in the traditional Syrian way—or go modern with a side of mashed potatoes.

Some say there was a custom of hiding a silver ring in one of the meatballs. Whoever found it was guaranteed good luck. This is not done today, but some defer to this tradition by hiding pine nuts in each meatball. This way anyone who eats this delicious dish has luck coming their way.

Kebabs

1 lb (500 g) lean ground lamb
    or beef
1 tsp salt, divided
½ tsp black pepper
¾ tsp *baharaat*
¼ tsp cinnamon
2 tbsp butter
⅓ cup (45 g) pine nuts

Sauce

4 tbsp olive oil
2 medium onions, julienned
½ cup (75 g) flour
3½ cups (800 g) stewed toma-
    toes, finely chopped
1 tbsp tomato paste
1 tsp *dibs rummaan* (optional)
¼ tsp sugar
2 tbsp chopped parsley
2 tbsp chopped mint

In a bowl, combine meat, ¾ tsp salt, pepper, *baharaat,* and cinnamon. Form into 30 to 35 small meatballs about the size of a hazelnut. Refrigerate.

In a large frying pan on medium-low heat, melt butter and toast pine nuts until golden, 3 to 4 minutes, stirring constantly. Remove pine nuts with a slotted spoon and set aside.

In the same frying pan on medium, heat oil and sauté onions until they're soft and begin to turn golden, about 8 minutes. Remove onions and set aside.

Dredge meatballs lightly in flour and fry them in the same frying pan on medium-low heat, carefully turning to brown evenly. Remove meatballs with a slotted spoon and set aside.

In the same frying pan, combine tomatoes, tomato paste, *dibs rummaan*, sugar, and ¼ tsp salt. Stir well, then add cooked onions. Cover and simmer for 15 minutes, then gently stir in meatballs. Cover and simmer for 30 minutes. Sprinkle pine nuts on top, along with parsley and mint. Cover and simmer for 5 minutes.

MAKES 6 SERVINGS

Kabaab Halabee

Aleppo Kebabs

Aleppo kebabs are distinct because they are covered and cooked with stewed tomatoes and onion spiced with Aleppo pepper. Serve this warm over *ruzz mufalfal* (see p. 54).

Kebabs

1 lb (500 g) ground lamb with a little fat

4 tbsp ground almonds

1 small onion, finely chopped

1½ tsp salt, divided

1 tsp *baharaat*

¼ tsp Aleppo pepper

Sauce

2 tbsp olive oil

1 large onion, halved and thinly sliced

3 cups (700 g) stewed tomatoes, finely chopped

2 tsp sumac

1 red bell pepper, seeded and julienned

Preheat oven to 350°F (180°C) degrees.

For the kebabs: In a bowl, thoroughly combine lamb, almonds, chopped onions, ½ tsp salt, *baharaat,* and Aleppo pepper. Then roll into 10 cylinders, 3 x 1 in (8 x 10 cm) in size, place evenly in a greased casserole dish, and set aside.

For the sauce: In a saucepan on medium-high, heat oil and sauté sliced onions until translucent, 4 to 5 minutes. Add stewed tomatoes and remaining salt and cook for 5 minutes. Stir in sumac and set aside.

Bake the kebabs for 15 minutes then remove from oven. Pour sauce evenly over kebabs and spread bell pepper on top. Bake for 30 minutes.

MAKES 10 KEBABS

Kabaab bil-Karaz

Meatballs and Cherries

Tourists from around the world may be drawn to Aleppo for its historic citadel, but the city's cuisine leaves an indelible impression. The cherries for this dish should be sour. Canned cherries are best but not the sweet, syrupy cherries used for pies and other desserts. Serve this hot over *ruzz mufalfal* (see p. 54) or *ruzz bi-sha'eereeya* (see p. 55).

1 lb (500 g) ground lamb or beef	1 tsp salt, divided
¼ cup (90 g) breadcrumbs	½ tsp black pepper, divided
2 eggs, beaten	1 large can pitted sour cherries
½ tsp allspice	(reserve juice)
½ tsp cumin	4 tbsp tomato paste
1 cup (150 g) very finely	1½ cups (375 mL) water
chopped onions, divided	2 tbsp olive oil

In a bowl, combine ground meat, breadcrumbs, egg, allspice, cumin, and ½ cup (75 g) onions, ½ tsp salt, and ¼ tsp pepper. Form into 30 1-in (2.5-cm) balls and set aside.

In a saucepan, combine meatballs, remaining onions, salt, and pepper, reserved cherry juice, tomato paste, water, and oil. Bring to a boil, reduce heat to medium-low, cover, and simmer for 40 minutes, stirring occasionally. Add cherries, reduce heat to low, cover, and simmer for 20 minutes, adding more water to cover if needed. Serve hot.

MAKES 30 MEATBALLS

Kafta Kabaab bil-Karaz

Barbecued Meatballs with Cherries

This unique dish uses a special type of small sour black cherry found only around Aleppo. In the mid-18th century, Alexander Russell noted that locals put onions, the bottoms of artichokes, or apple slices between the pieces of meat. Serve this hot with *ruzz mufalfal* (see p. 54).

1 lb (500 g) finely ground lean
    lamb
¾ tsp salt
½ tsp black pepper
½ tsp allspice
½ tsp cumin

½ tsp coriander
¼ tsp cinnamon
¼ tsp nutmeg
⅛ tsp Aleppo pepper
large pitted fresh or canned
    sour cherries

In a food processor, blend all ingredients except cherries for 1 minute. Form 30 small balls, about 1 in (2.5 cm) in diameter, wetting your hands to keep meat from sticking.

On metal skewers, place together tightly, one meatball, one cherry, one meatball, one cherry, until there are five of each. Then slightly press each ball to secure the meat on the skewer.

Grill until meat is no longer pink, 5 to 10 minutes.

MAKES 30 MEATBALLS

Kafta

Grilled Ground Meat

Aleppo is the home of the best *kafta* in the world, known for its vivid flavors and well-blended spices. Perhaps *kafta* originated in Aleppo and traveled the Silk Road to Xi'an, China, where Habeeb enjoyed the spicy, juicy barbecued ground meat of Shaanxi province.

2 lb (900 g) leg of lamb with a little fat, ground twice or processed until very smooth	1½ tsp salt
	¾ tsp black pepper
	1 tsp *baharaat*
1 medium onion, chopped	½ tsp cumin
1 large red bell pepper, seeded and chopped	¼ tsp cinnamon
	¼ tsp Aleppo pepper
2 cups (50 g) finely chopped parsley	4 tbsp pine nuts, toasted
	4 tbsp butter for brushing

In a bowl, combine all ingredients except pine nuts and butter. In a food processor, blend mixture until smooth. Transfer to a bowl and mix in pine nuts.

Divide meat mixture into 18 balls, then wrap each ball around a metal skewer and shape into a large cigar, about 1½ in (4 cm) thick.

Place skewers on an oiled grill for 4 minutes on each side, brushing all over occasionally with butter.

Serve immediately with grilled tomatoes atop a platter of rice. These *kafta* are best eaten pulled off the skewers and wrapped in *marqouq*.

MAKES 18 KAFTA

Kafta Shaameeya

Damascus Kafta

This is Damascus's answer to meatloaf. The juice from the tomatoes infuses the meat, enhancing the spices and herbs.

1 lb (500 g) ground lamb or beef

1 cup (100 g) finely ground
    walnuts

2 medium onions, finely
    chopped

2 garlic cloves, crushed

4 tbsp finely chopped cilantro

1 tsp dried mint, crushed

1 tsp salt

½ tsp allspice

½ tsp black pepper

2 medium tomatoes, thinly
    sliced

2 tbsp olive oil

Preheat oven to 350°F (180°C).

In a mixing bowl, combine all ingredients except tomatoes and oil. Spread evenly in a greased casserole dish, then place tomato slices over top. Drizzle with oil. Bake for 1 hour or until meat is no longer pink inside. Remove from the oven as soon as it's ready and serve immediately.

MAKES 6 SERVINGS

Kafta Mabrouma

Coiled *Kafta* with Pine Nuts

This is a speciality of Aleppo, where it is baked and served on a round platter with the rolls arranged in diminishing concentric circles.

2 medium onions, very finely chopped

4 garlic cloves, crushed

1 egg, beaten

2 lb (900 g) finely ground lean lamb

2 tsp salt

1 tsp black pepper

½ tsp allspice

¼ tsp cayenne

4 tbsp pine nuts

2 tbsp melted butter

2 tbsp water

2 tbsp roughly chopped parsley

1 lemon, sliced

Preheat oven to 300°F (150°C).

In a mixing bowl, thoroughly combine onions, garlic, egg, lamb, salt, pepper, allspice, and cayenne. On a clean surface, flatten mixture to about ¼ in (6 mm) thickness, then cut into 6 even rectangles. Divide pine nuts into six portions and press into the longer side of each piece. Roll into a sausage shape and then gently form into a crescent. Arrange rolls tightly in a spiral in a round casserole dish, then brush with butter and sprinkle with water. Cover and bake for 40 minutes, then uncover and bake for 20 minutes, or until rolls are no longer pink inside.

Place on a warmed serving platter, then garnish with parsley and lemon slices. Serve with *ruzz mufalfal* (see p. 54) or fried potatoes.

MAKES 6 TO 8 SERVINGS

Kubba Qaraas
Deep-Fried Stuffed Kibbeh

There are 30 (some say 100!) types of kibbeh in Aleppo alone. *Kubba* means "ball," and *qaraas* means "patties," which is a bit misleading, as they are often shaped like eggs. Ingredients vary depending on region; for example, *dibs rummaan*, quince, sumac, and cherry juice are additions unique to Aleppo. An 1889 American newspaper wrote that kibbeh is "to Syria what pork and beans are to New England." A 1905 article described it as holding "the place in the Syrian menu that turkey does on the American." In Brazil, *kibe* is a fast food as popular as hamburgers are in North America.

In the 18th and 19th centuries, the women of Syrian households would spend at least half a day preparing kibbeh together, taking turns pounding the meat and onions into a paste with a pestle in a large stone mortar. It was an assembly line of kibbeh makers—some forming the balls, others filling them, and still others closing them. In a small mountain village in Syria, we were served this *kubba* stuffing in a unique manner—sitting hot atop a dish of *hummus bi-taheena* (see p. 83). Delicious!

Kubba stuffing
3 tbsp butter
½ lb (250 g) ground lamb or beef
¼ cup (35 g) toasted pine nuts
    or coarsely chopped walnuts
1 medium onion, finely chopped
½ tsp salt
¼ tsp nutmeg
¼ tsp allspice
¼ tsp black pepper

Kubba
1½ cups (340 g) fine (#1) bulgur

1½ lb (750 g) lean leg of lamb,
    cut into 2-in (5-cm) cubes
2 medium onions, finely
    chopped
1½ tsp salt
1 tsp dried mint, crushed
1 tsp black pepper
1 tsp cumin
1 tsp allspice
½ tsp cinnamon
⅛ tsp cayenne or Aleppo pepper
vegetable oil for deep-frying

Continues...

Soak bulgur in warm water for 20 minutes, then press water out through a fine mesh strainer.

For the stuffing: In a frying pan on medium heat, melt butter and sauté meat for 3 minutes or until it begins to brown. Stir in remaining ingredients, then sauté for 8 minutes or until onions are soft. Set aside.

For the *kubba:* In a food processor, grind lamb cubes, then add remaining ingredients except bulgur and process into a firm paste. Place in a mixing bowl and knead the bulgur into the paste until completely blended. Process mixture again.

Scoop up a ball of paste about the size of a golf ball and place in the palm of one hand. Use the forefinger of the other hand to make and indentation. Expand the hollow by rotating and pressing the ball against the palm of your hand until the shell is about ¼ in (6 mm) thick. Place one heaping tablespoon of stuffing in the hollow and close it up and form into an egg shape. Slightly dip your fingers in a bowl of cold water with a sprinkling of salt to help smooth it out.

In a saucepan on medium-high, heat oil and deep-fry kibbeh for 3 to 4 minutes or until golden brown. Drain on paper towel.

Serve hot with a dish of yogurt.

MAKES 20 TO 22 KIBBEH

Kubba Maseelouqaat Kubbaybaat

Boiled Kibbeh

This unique traditional kibbeh is boiled and accompanied by a tangy sauce. Our version has meat, whereas in northwestern Syria a Lenten type is made with a bulgur shell stuffed with spinach and onions.

½ cup (115 g) fine (#1) bulgur

¼ lb (125 g) ground lamb

½ large onion, grated

1 tsp *baharaat*

½ tsp salt

½ tsp black pepper

1 cup (200 g) *kubba* stuffing (see p. 168)

¼ cup (60 mL) water

½ cup (50 g) coarsely ground walnuts

¼ cup (60 mL) lemon juice

½ cup (125 mL) olive oil

1 tsp *dibs rummaan*

½ cup (15 g) finely chopped parsley

1 tsp dried mint, crushed

⅛ tsp cayenne

2 garlic cloves, crushed

3 tbsp crushed roasted red bell pepper

Soak bulgur in water to cover for 1 hour, then press water out through a fine mesh strainer.

In a food processor, blend bulgur, lamb, and onions for 2 minutes. Transfer

Continues...

to a bowl and mix in *baharaat*, salt, and pepper by hand.

Form mixture into 7 balls. Hold a ball in the palm of one hand, then use the forefinger of the other hand to make an indentation. Expand the hollow by rotating and pressing the ball against the palm of your hand until the shell is about ¼ in (6 mm) thick. Place one heaping tablespoon of stuffing into the hollow and then close it up to form into an egg shape. Slightly dip your fingers in a bowl of cold water with a sprinkling of salt to help smooth it out.

In a saucepan, bring enough water to cover the kibbeh to a boil. Gently place kibbeh in water, bring to a boil, reduce heat to medium, and cook for 20 minutes. Remove kibbeh and place on a serving platter.

In a mixing bowl, combine ¼ cup (60 mL) water and walnuts. Add lemon, oil, *dibs rummaan*, parsley, mint, cayenne, garlic, and bell pepper. Drizzle over kibbeh and serve.

MAKES 7 KIBBEH

Kubba Labaneeya

Kibbeh in Yogurt Sauce

Savory fried kibbeh, cooked in tart and creamy *labaneeya*.

2 cups (500 mL) yogurt mixed
    with 2 cups (500 mL) water
1 tbsp cornstarch diluted in ¼
    cup (60 mL) water
1 egg, beaten
1 tsp salt

½ tsp black pepper
12 prepared *kubba qaraas* (see
    p. 168)
2 tbsp butter
6 garlic cloves, crushed
1 tbsp dried mint

In a saucepan on medium heat, cook yogurt-water mixture, stirring continuously in one direction to prevent curdling until it comes to a gentle boil. Stir in diluted cornstarch and continue stirring until heated through, about 1 minute. Stir in egg and bring to a gentle boil. Remove from heat and stir in salt and pepper.

Add *kubba qaraas* to yogurt sauce and on medium-low heat bring to a gentle boil, stirring occasionally. Transfer to a serving bowl.

In a frying pan on medium heat, melt butter and sauté garlic for 1 minute. Add mint and sauté for 30 seconds. Spoon garlic mixture over *kubba labaneeya* and serve immediately.

MAKES 4 SERVINGS

Kubba Haamid

Kibbeh in Lemon Sauce

Habeeb's family enjoyed this kibbeh cooked in a tart, lemony sauce for years on their farm. Sometimes it was made with bulgur and flour instead of meat, but this "imposter" version was also a favorite. Shams's generation was probably the last to habitually make this traditional Syrian kibbeh. Now, grilled or fried tends to be the preferred method.

Kubba

1 lb (500 g) lean ground beef or lamb

½ cup (115 g) fine (#1) bulgur

1 medium onion, finely chopped

1 tsp salt

½ tsp dried mint, crushed

½ tsp black pepper

½ tsp cumin

½ tsp allspice

¼ tsp cinnamon

⅛ tsp cayenne

Lemon sauce

½ lb (250 g) lamb shoulder, cut into ½-in (1-cm) cubes

2 tsp salt

1 tsp nutmeg

1 tsp allspice

½ tsp black pepper

8 cups (2 L) water

1 large onion, finely chopped

1 19-oz (540-mL) can chickpeas, drained

4 garlic cloves, crushed

½ cup (125 mL) lemon juice

Soak bulgur in warm water for 15 minutes, then press water out through a fine mesh strainer.

For the *kubba:* In a food processor, grind meat for 3 minutes, then add remaining *kubba* ingredients and process for 1 minute. Form into marble-sized balls and set aside.

For the sauce: In a saucepan, bring all ingredients for the lemon sauce except lemon juice to a boil, then reduce heat to medium-low, cover, and cook for 30 minutes. Add *kubba* balls, cover, and cook for 40 minutes. Add lemon juice, cover, and cook for 15 minutes.

MAKES 8 SERVINGS

Kubba bil-Saneeya

Kibbeh Pie

For a busy cook, this is the easiest kibbeh to make.

1 recipe *kubba qaraas* mixture (see p. 168)

1 recipe *kubba* stuffing (see p. 168)

¼ cup (60 mL) olive oil

Prepare *kubba qaraas* mixture and set aside.

Preheat oven to 350°F (180°C).

Divide *kubba qaraas* mixture into 2 equal portions. Spread one portion on the bottom of a greased 9 x 13-in (3.5-L) casserole dish. Spread *kubba* stuffing evenly over top, then spread remaining portion of *kubba qaraas* mixture over stuffing. Cut into 2 x 2-in (5 x 5-cm) diamonds or squares, then drizzle oil over top.

Bake for 40 minutes and serve.

MAKES 6 TO 8 SERVINGS

Mansaf

A Dish of Hospitality

Each family may have its own regional or personal variation of *mansaf*, some using chicken instead of lamb, others preparing two types of kibbeh instead of one, and still others placing the lamb on the outer edges of the serving platter because the guest is so honored and welcome that no effort should be needed to reach for a piece of meat.

Jabal al-Arab is a mountainous region of volcanic rock in the southernmost part of Syria that is known for *mansaf*, its dish of hospitality. *Mansaf* is a sign of welcome, a dish of luxury served to honored guests and dignitaries. At the same time, folklore describes it as the link between rich and poor—the meat of wealth and the bulgur of poverty, sitting together as equals. *Mansaf* is also the connection between the past and the present, a Syrian dish that has been carried down through the generations. If you have the good fortune to watch this dish being prepared in someone's home in Jabal al-Arab, you will hear the women sing songs about it as they cook and then watch the men carry it out in a large tray. Perhaps this is why it is called the "dish of men"—so big and heavy is the traditional platter that not one but two men must serve it.

2 lb (900 g) lamb shoulder or leg, cut into large cubes

1 large onion, halved

2 tsp salt, divided

1 tsp black pepper, divided

6 cups (1.5 L) yogurt

2 tbsp cornstarch

2 tsp turmeric

¼ tsp saffron threads, crushed

¼ cup (60 mL) water

2 beef bouillon cubes

¼ cup (60 mL) *labna* (see p. 58)

2 tsp dried marjoram, crushed

3 cups (700 g) coarse (#3 or #4) bulgur

1 cup (250 mL) clarified butter

4 tbsp pine nuts, toasted in butter

½ recipe cooked *kubba qaraas* (see p. 168)

Continues...

meat · 177

In a large saucepan, cover lamb, onions, 1 tsp salt, and ½ tsp pepper with 2 in (5 cm) water and bring to a boil. Reduce heat to medium-low, cover, and simmer for 1 hour. Remove lamb and set aside. Strain the broth into a bowl and reserve.

In another saucepan on medium, heat yogurt until it comes to a boil. You must have patience to prepare the sauce, as it must be stirred gently and continuously in one direction so that the yogurt doesn't curdle. Mix cornstarch, turmeric, and saffron with ¼ cup water. Stir into yogurt, reduce heat to low, and cook for 5 minutes, stirring until well blended and smooth. Add bouillon cubes and *labna* and stir until sauce begins to thicken. Add ½ cup (125 mL) reserved lamb broth, keeping the sauce thick but allowing the broth flavor to be absorbed in the sauce. Stir in marjoram and remaining salt and pepper. Add lamb, increase heat to medium-low, and cook for 10 minutes, stirring constantly.

While the meat is cooking in the yogurt sauce, in a large saucepan bring bulgur and 6 cups (1.5 L) reserved lamb broth to a boil, then reduce heat to low, cover, and cook for 15 minutes, stirring occasionally, covering the saucepan again each time.

In a saucepan, melt clarified butter, then stir into cooked bulgur. Carefully scoop out 2 cups (500 mL) of the yogurt sauce (without the lamb) and gently stir it into the cooked bulgur until well blended. Transfer bulgur to a large round serving platter. Place lamb pieces on top and garnish with pine nuts. Place *kubba qaraas* (see p. 168) around the edges of the platter. Each diner should have a bowl of yogurt sauce to accompany the *mansaf*.

MAKES 8 TO 10 SERVINGS

Shish Barak

Dumplings in Yogurt

Once there was a married couple, the husband much older than the wife. One day she was in the kitchen, trying to create a new dish for dinner, while her old and feeble husband was sitting in his chair. She was worried about him and began to mutter: "*Shih, shih barak*," a colloquial Damascene expression meaning, "The shah, the shah is sitting." At that point, her son came into the kitchen and asked about this new dish she was making. She didn't notice him and continued muttering the same words over and over. Her son thought she was answering his question and walked away believing this was the name of the dish: *shish barak*.

Dumplings

1 lb (500 g) fresh or frozen (and thawed) pizza or bread dough

2 tbsp butter

1 lb (500 g) ground lamb or beef

4 tbsp pine nuts or slivered almonds

½ tsp salt

½ tsp black pepper

½ tsp coriander

¼ tsp cinnamon

½ tsp *baharaat*

2 medium onions, finely chopped

2 garlic cloves, minced

Yogurt sauce

2 eggs, beaten

3 cups (700 mL) yogurt

3 cups (700 mL) cold water

2 tbsp butter

2 garlic cloves, crushed

1 tsp salt

2 tbsp dried mint

For the dumplings: Form dough into ¾-in (2-cm) balls, cover with a tea towel, and let rest for 1 hour.

Meanwhile, make the filling. In a pan on medium heat, melt butter and sauté meat until light brown, then add remaining dumpling ingredients and stir-fry for 5 minutes. Set aside.

Preheat oven to 350°F (180°C).

Roll out dough balls to make circles ⅛ in (3 mm) thick. Place 1 level teaspoon filling on each circle, then fold dough over filling and pinch edges to seal. Fold in half again to shape dumpling like a thimble and pinch to close. Place dumplings on a greased baking tray and bake for 10 minutes or until lightly browned, turning once, then set aside.

For the yogurt sauce: In a saucepan on medium heat, stir eggs and yogurt until well blended. Add cold water and stir well. Stir continuously in one direction until mixture comes to a gentle boil, then reduce heat to low.

Meanwhile, in a small saucepan on medium heat, melt butter. Add garlic, salt, and mint and sauté for 2 minutes or until garlic turns golden brown, then mix garlic mixture into yogurt sauce.

Place dumplings in sauce, cover, and cook on medium-low heat for 15 minutes.

Serve piping hot.

MAKES 8 SERVINGS

A nickname for this dish in Aleppo is *udhanayn* (ears), to evoke the curved shape of the dumplings.

Al-Baasha wa 'Asaakirhu

The Pasha and His Soldiers

This luxurious Damascene dish goes back to the Ottoman occupation. *Shish barak* (see p. 179) dumplings are the soldiers guarding the pasha—*kubba qaraas* (see p. 168)—cooked together in a yogurt sauce. Some Syrians give the same name to *daawoud baasha* (see p. 160).

½ recipe *kubba qaraas* mixture (see p. 168)

Dumplings

½ lb (250 g) fresh or frozen (and thawed) pizza or bread dough

1 tbsp butter

¼ lb (125 g) ground lamb or beef

2 tbsp pine nuts or slivered almonds

½ tsp salt

½ tsp black pepper

½ tsp coriander

¼ tsp cinnamon

½ tsp *baharaat*

1 medium onion, finely chopped

2 garlic cloves, minced

Yogurt sauce

2 eggs, beaten

4 cups (1 L) yogurt

4 cups (1 L) cold water

2 tbsp butter

4 garlic cloves, crushed

1 tsp salt

1 tbsp dried mint

Continues...

Prepare *kubba qaraas,* form into walnut-sized balls, and deep-fry. Set aside.

For the dumplings: Form dough into ¾-in (2-cm) balls, then cover with a tea towel and let rest for 1 hour.

Preheat oven to 350°F (180°C).

Meanwhile, make the filling. In a frying pan on medium, melt butter and sauté meat for 5 minutes, until it begins to brown, then add remaining dumpling ingredients and sauté for 5 minutes. Set aside.

Roll out dough balls to make circles ⅛ in (3 mm) thick. Place 1 level tsp filling on each circle, then fold dough over filling and pinch edges to seal. Fold in half again to shape dumpling like a thimble and pinch to close. Place dumplings on a greased baking tray, bake for 15 minutes, then set aside.

For the yogurt sauce: In a large saucepan, stir eggs and yogurt until well blended. Add water and stir well. Cook on medium heat, gently stirring in one direction to prevent curdling, until mixture comes to a soft boil, then reduce heat to low.

Meanwhile, in a small saucepan on medium heat, melt butter. Add garlic, salt, and mint and sauté until garlic just begins to brown. Remove from heat and stir saucepan contents into yogurt sauce.

To complete the dish, place dumplings and kibbeh balls in yogurt sauce, cover, and cook on medium-low heat for 15 minutes. Transfer to a large bowl and serve piping hot.

MAKES 10 TO 12 SERVINGS

Kousa Mihshee bil-Laban

Stuffed Zucchini in Yogurt

Syrians love their *mihshee* (stuffed) dishes and have brought them everywhere. A 1903 American newspaper article about New York's Little Syria notes, "A favorite dish is vegetable marrow scooped out and filled with finely chopped meat rolled in rice." Any little zucchini or small tender green squash can be used for this dish.

Zucchini

Stuffed zucchini

½ cup (100 g) basmati or other long-grain white rice

8 zucchini, about 6 in (15 cm) long

1 medium onion, finely chopped

4 tbsp butter

¼ cup (35 g) pine nuts, lightly toasted

½ lb (250 g) ground lamb

4 tbsp finely chopped cilantro

1 tsp salt

1 tsp *baharaat*

½ tsp allspice

½ tsp black pepper

¼ tsp cinnamon

pinch of cayenne

Yogurt sauce

3 cups (700 mL) yogurt

1½ cups (375 mL) cold water

2 tbsp butter

6 garlic cloves, crushed

¾ tsp salt

1 tbsp dried mint

Continues...

For the stuffed zucchini: Soak rice for 30 minutes, then rinse and drain thoroughly to avoid starch buildup that would make the stuffing pasty.

Cut off the tops of zucchini and reserve. Core zucchini, taking care not to tear the skin. The secret is patience. The result should be a thin, even vegetable shell.

In a bowl, thoroughly mix rice and remaining stuffing ingredients. Stuff zucchini ¾ full, since rice expands when cooked. Place reserved tops over openings.

In a large saucepan, arrange zucchini in layers and barely cover with water. Place an inverted plate on top, bring to a boil, reduce heat to medium-low, cover, and simmer for 1 hour or until tender.

For the yogurt sauce: In a saucepan, stir yogurt and water until well blended. On medium heat, gently stir continuously in one direction until mixture comes to boil to prevent curdling. Reduce heat to very low.

In a frying pan on medium heat, melt butter then add garlic, salt, and mint. Sauté for 2 minutes or until garlic begins to brown, then stir garlic mixture into yogurt. Remove sauce from heat but keep warm.

Once zucchini is cooked, uncover, remove plate, and pour yogurt sauce over top. Cook on medium-low heat for 15 minutes. Serve hot with *salatat soureeya* (see p. 133).

MAKES 4 SERVINGS

Yabraq

Meat-Stuffed Grape Leaves

The Ottomans are given credit for introducing stuffed grape leaves to Syria, since *yabraq* is the Turkish word for grapevine. But we need to give the Syrians credit for perfecting these delicious finger-shaped rolls. *Yabraq* is always served with yogurt, as there is nothing tastier than hot grape leaves dipped in cold yogurt.

2 lb (900 g) ground lamb or veal

2 cups (400 g) basmati or other long-grain white rice

2 tsp salt

1¾ tsp black pepper

1¼ tsp cinnamon

⅛ tsp Aleppo pepper

1 tsp allspice

½ cup (113 g) butter, at room temperature, divided

1 16-oz (454-g) jar preserved grape leaves, or equivalent amount of fresh leaves

3 medium potatoes, peeled and thinly sliced

⅓ cup (80 mL) lemon juice mixed with 4 garlic cloves, crushed

For the stuffing: in a bowl, combine meat, rice, salt, black pepper, cinnamon, Aleppo pepper, allspice, and ¼ cup (57 g) butter.

If using preserved grape leaves, drain them, then place in a bowl and cover with boiling water. Let sit for 15 minutes, then rinse and drain in colander. If using fresh leaves, place in a bowl and cover with boiling water and let sit for 1 minute. Trim stems and shake off any excess water. Place a few grape leaves on a flat work surface, shiny side down with the stem end facing you.

Continues...

Place one heaping teaspoon of stuffing (depending on size of leaf) length-wise at bottom of leaf but not touching the edges. Roll grape leaf over filling, folding in the edges after the first roll. Continue until all leaves are rolled.

In a large saucepan, place potato slices along bottom in one even layer. This prevents the rolls from sticking to the bottom. Place rolled grape leaves seam side down over potato slices, arranging them in tight, compact rows, alternating direction with each row.

Place an inverted plate over rolls, pressing down slightly, to keep rolls intact. Cover with enough water to almost reach the top of the plate. Cover and cook on medium heat for 50 minutes or until leaves are tender and rice is cooked. Remove plate and reduce heat to medium-low. Pour lemon-garlic mixture over top, cover, and cook for 10 minutes. Remove from heat and let stand for 10 minutes.

MAKES 6 TO 8 SERVINGS

If there is leftover filling, you can core a few small tomatoes, stuff them, cover with the tomato tops, and put them in the pot on top of the rolled leaves. Leila freezes leftover filling, though there usually isn't much, if any.

Mihshee Malfouf

Cabbage Rolls

The Syrian version of cabbage rolls is garlicky and spicy, cooked with either tomato juice or lemon juice and water. This variation is Habeeb's favorite—following in his mother's footsteps, he adds a finely chopped onion to the stuffing for extra zing.

1 medium cabbage, about 3 lb (1.5 kg)	4 tbsp finely chopped cilantro
1 lb (500 g) lamb or beef, ground or cut into very small pieces	1 tsp black pepper
1 medium onion, finely chopped	½ tsp allspice
1 cup (200 g) basmati or other long-grain white rice, rinsed and drained	½ tsp cumin
	½ tsp cinnamon
	⅛ tsp cayenne
2 cups (450 g) stewed tomatoes, finely chopped	1½ tsp salt
4 tbsp melted butter	8 garlic cloves, chopped into large pieces
4 tbsp finely chopped mint	2 cups (500 mL) tomato juice, mixed with 1 tsp salt and 1 tsp dried oregano

In a pot of boiling water, cook whole cabbage for 2 to 3 minutes to soften leaves. Loosen leaves from the stem with a knife. Cut out thick ribs and slice large leaves in half. If inner leaves are not yet soft, boil again for 1 to 2 minutes. Set leaves aside and reserve ribs.

For the stuffing: in a mixing bowl combine remaining ingredients except garlic and tomato juice.

Continues...

Place some stuffing on the bottom end of a cabbage leaf and roll, tucking in edges while rolling. Continue until all leaves are stuffed.

In a saucepan, cover bottom with trimmed ribs and torn leaves. Arrange rolls side by side in alternating layers, placing garlic pieces between rolls. Pour in tomato juice, then cover with an inverted plate. Add enough water to just cover the plate.

Bring to a boil, reduce heat to medium-low, cover, and cook for 1¼ hours.

Carefully remove the plate covering the cabbage rolls. Either serve cabbage rolls directly from the saucepan or carefully transfer to a serving dish. Serve hot.

MAKES 8 SERVINGS

Makmour al-Malfouf

Lamb and Rice Wrapped in Cabbage

Makmour means "wrapped," as the rice is cooked with the cabbage wrapped around it.

Makmour al-malfouf is a generations-old dish passed down from our great-great-grandparents, especially popular in rural Syria, where it is one of the first dishes a mother teaches her daughter to prepare. It is a *sha'bee* dish—a people's meal, since the ingredients are readily available year round—and a great way to get kids to eat their vegetables.

½ tbsp olive oil

¾ lb (375 g) ground lamb

6 garlic cloves, minced

1½ tsp salt, divided

1 tsp black pepper, divided

1¼ tsp cumin, divided

¾ tsp *baharaat*

1 tsp dried mint, crushed, divided

3 tbsp *dibs rummaan,* divided

4 cups (400 g) thinly sliced cabbage

1 cup (200 g) basmati or other long-grain white rice, soaked for 1 hour then drained

3¼ cups (770 mL) boiling water

In a deep saucepan on medium-low, heat oil and cook lamb for 5 minutes, stirring frequently. Add garlic, ¾ tsp salt, ½ tsp black pepper, ¾ tsp cumin, *baharaat,* ½ tsp mint, and 1½ tbsp *dibs rummaan.* Mix well and cook for 10 minutes, or until meat is browned.

Stir in cabbage and remaining salt, pepper, cumin, mint, and *dibs*

Continues...

rummaan, increase heat to medium, and cook until cabbage is soft, about 15 minutes, stirring frequently.

Push cabbage mixture to the sides of the saucepan, add rice in the middle, then turn the cabbage over the rice. Pour in boiling water, reduce heat to medium-low, cover, and cook for 20 to 25 minutes.

Remove from heat and let sit for 10 minutes before serving.

MAKES 6 TO 8 SERVINGS

Baasamshakaat

The Bride of Damascus

In Damascus, the traditional method of sewing the rolls shut or tying them with string is slowly disappearing. The modern Syrian cook will wrap the stuffed meat rolls in tinfoil, prick them a few times, and cook them in boiling water for about 1 1/2 hours. Then they are unwrapped, simmered in sauce, and served.

These rolls of lean meat stuffed with rice, diced or ground meat, and spices are one of the best of Damascus's traditional dishes. It's unclear where the alluring name for this dish came from, but that just makes it more enticing. Serve this with *ruzz mufalfal* (see p. 54).

8 tbsp butter, divided
1 medium onion, finely chopped
2 cups ground lamb or beef
½ tsp salt
2 tsp *baharaat,* divided
1 cup (250 g) cooked basmati or other long-grain white rice

2 lb steak, pounded thin and cut into 6 x 4-in (15 x 10-cm) rectangles
4 tbsp olive oil
2 large onions, julienned
2 cups (450 g) stewed tomatoes
2 tbsp tomato paste
2 cups (500 mL) beef stock

In a frying pan on medium-high heat, melt 2 tbsp butter and sauté chopped onions until soft, about 5 minutes. Add ground meat, salt, and 1 tsp *baharaat,* then brown the meat and continue to sauté until cooked through, about 8 minutes.

Stir in rice and cook for 1 minute, then remove from heat. Divide filling according to the number of portions of steak.

Place one filling portion on the narrower bottom end of a piece of steak and roll tightly. Secure roll with kitchen twine, packing in any loose filling. Repeat with remaining filling and steak pieces.

In a large frying pan on medium-high heat, melt 6 tbsp butter and place

Continues...

meat rolls side by side in the pan. Brown rolls on all sides, then cover with water and bring to a boil. Reduce heat to medium and cook for 30 minutes.

While rolls are cooking, in a deep frying pan on medium, heat oil and sauté julienned onions until soft, about 8 minutes. Add remaining ingredients, including 1 tsp *baharaat*. Cook, stirring occasionally, until sauce thickens, about 10 minutes.

Remove meat rolls from liquid and add to sauce, reduce heat to medium-low, cover, and cook for 15 minutes.

Spoon half the sauce onto a serving platter and arrange the *baasam-shakaat* on top. Serve with remaining sauce on the side.

MAKES 8 SERVINGS

Maqlouba

Upside-Down Lamb and Rice

Many nations lay claim to this succulent one-pot meal, but it is the Palestinians who take the most pride in its origins. For it was when the great leader Saladin regained the holy city of Jerusalem from the Crusaders that the link between *maqlouba* and Palestine took hold. To celebrate the victory, the city's inhabitants presented the dish in the traditional way—the contents of the pot flipped over onto the serving tray before the guests. Saladin enjoyed the dish so much he named it *al-maqlouba*, "that which is turned over."

1½ lb (500 g) eggplant
1 tsp salt, divided
1½ tbsp olive oil
1½ lb (750 g) leg of lamb, cubed
½ tsp black pepper
½ tsp *baharaat*
¼ tsp cinnamon
¼ tsp coriander
pinch of Aleppo pepper
2 bay leaves
2 tbsp butter, divided
vegetable oil for deep-frying

1 red bell pepper, seeded and julienned
1 yellow (or green) bell pepper, seeded and julienned
1 medium onion, julienned
1 medium tomato, skin removed, sliced thinly
1½ cups (300 g) basmati or other long-grain white rice, soaked for 30 minutes then drained
2¼ cups (530 mL) boiling water

Continues...

Peel eggplant, cut into 1-in (2.5-cm) cubes, salt lightly, and let sit in a colander overnight to drain its water.

In a large saucepan on medium-high, heat oil and sauté lamb for 10 minutes, until meat has browned. Add ¾ tsp salt, black pepper, *baharaat*, cinnamon, coriander, and Aleppo pepper. Sauté for 2 minutes, then add bay leaves and cover with 1 in (2.5 cm) water. Bring to a boil, reduce heat to medium-low, cover, and cook until lamb is tender, about 50 minutes, stirring often. Uncover, discard bay leaves, and cook on medium-high to reduce the water, about 10 to 15 minutes. Add 1 tbsp butter and stir for 1 to 2 minutes.

While meat is cooking, deep-fry eggplant until golden and drain on paper towels. Deep-fry bell peppers, then onions, and drain on paper towels. Set aside until ready to use, changing paper towels once.

In the saucepan, arrange eggplant evenly on top of meat. Then arrange bell peppers on top, then onions, and then tomatoes. Add rice and gently pat it down and spread it evenly. Add remaining butter and pour in boiling water. Bring to a boil on medium, reduce heat to low, cover and cook for 35 minutes. If needed add a little more water to ensure rice is cooked. Remove from heat and let sit for 5 minutes.

Place a round serving dish over top of the pot and flip both the pot and the dish upside down. Gently remove the pot to dislodge, pressing any loose ingredients back into shape.

Serve immediately with yogurt and *salatat soureeya* (see p. 133).

MAKES 4 TO 6 SERVINGS

Shalbaatou

Lamb and Kohlrabi with Rice

According to Damascenes, *shalbaatou* is nearly two centuries old—and *"Tadub feehaa al-baraka,"* the blessing infuses it. It makes for a nourishing, yet thrifty meal, with a unique flavor from the kohlrabi. In the Palestinian village of Az-Zeeb, razed by Israeli forces in 1948, *shalbaatou* was a popular dish made with eggplant, tomatoes, and bulgur, which Palestinians still prepare.

8 tbsp butter, divided

¾ cup (85 g) blanched slivered almonds

½ cup (70 g) pine nuts

1 lb (500 g) lean lamb cut into ¼-in (6-mm) cubes

1 tsp salt

1 tsp black pepper

4 tsp beef broth powder

2 large kohlrabi, peeled, thinly sliced, cut into small pieces, and sprinkled with salt

1 cup (150 g) finely chopped carrots

2 cups (400 g) basmati or other long-grain white rice, soaked in hot water for 30 minutes then drained

2¼ cups (530 mL) boiling water

In a frying pan on medium-low heat, melt 2 tbsp butter and sauté almonds and pine nuts until golden. Set pan aside and keep warm.

In a large saucepan on medium heat, melt 4 tbsp butter and sauté lamb until it begins to brown, 10 to 12 minutes. Mix in salt, pepper, and broth powder, and sauté for 2 to 3 minutes. Add kohlrabi and carrots and sauté for 5 minutes. Stir in rice and sauté for 1 minute. Add water and remaining 2 tbsp butter,

Continues...

stir, and bring to a boil. Reduce heat to medium-low, cover, and cook for 12 minutes. Remove from heat and let sit for 15 minutes.

Transfer to a serving platter and decorate with toasted nuts, drizzling over any butter left in the pan.

MAKES 6 TO 8 SERVINGS

Hareesa

A Creamy Comfort Dish of Lamb and Rice

Hareesa is a Syrian dish that has been carried forward from ancient times. Of humble origin but rich in taste, historically it was popular with everyone, from peasants to nobles, and is served for weddings, special occasions, and Ramadan. *Hareesa* is typically much less spicy than our version, Habeeb loves his spices! Serve this with *laban* (see p. 56) and *lift* (see p. 89). Scoop up every morsel with Arab bread.

1½ cups (300 g) basmati or other long-grain white rice

1¼ gal (5 L) water, divided

2 lb (900 g) bone-in lamb shoulder pieces, or other bone-in cut of lamb (steaks, chops, or shanks), about 8 pieces

½ tsp cumin

½ tsp coriander

½ tsp ground ginger

½ tsp cinnamon

¼ tsp cayenne

generous pinch freshly grated nutmeg

generous pinch ground cloves

2 tsp salt

3 tbsp melted unsalted butter

In a bowl, soak rice in 10 cups (2.5 L) of water for 4 hours.

In a stockpot, bring lamb, spices, and remaining 10 cups (2.5 L) water to a boil. Reduce heat to medium-low and cook, removing any froth, for 2½ hours or until meat is very tender and falling off the bone, adding more water to cover, if necessary.

Add soaked rice with its water and salt to the stockpot. Cook for 1 hour,

Continues...

or until rice and lamb become tender, similar to a smooth porridge, stirring often and adding more water if necessary.

Remove from heat and allow to cool. Remove and discard bones.

In a food processor, grind saucepan contents to a paste. Return paste to the stockpot and reheat on low, stirring constantly.

Place in individual bowls, drizzle with butter, and serve.

MAKES 8 SERVINGS

Ouzi

The Daughter of Damascus

Ouzi is a well-known, luxurious dish in Damascus, Aleppo, and the surrounding areas. No iftar table to break the Ramadan fast or wedding banquet is complete without this rich, festive dish. *Ouzi* originally referred to what we now use as the stuffing for these pies and was served spread out on a huge platter at weddings, where the guests would scoop it up by hand. This way of eating cultivated kinship, but it was very untidy; hence, the idea to create individual pies filled with *ouzi*. Serve warm with *shaneena* (see p. 333), *laban* (see p. 56), or *khiyaar bil-laban* (see p. 140) so that yogurt can ease the digestion of such a luxurious dish.

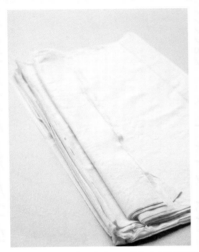

Phyllo

4 tbsp olive oil

1 cup (250 g) ground lamb

1 medium onion, finely chopped

4 garlic cloves, minced

4 tbsp finely chopped cilantro

1 tsp salt

½ tsp black pepper

½ tsp cumin

½ tsp allspice

¼ tsp ground cinnamon

⅛ tsp Aleppo pepper

1 cup (150 g) fresh or frozen peas

2 cups (500 g) cooked basmati or other long-grain white rice

½ cup (70 g) pine nuts or slivered almonds, toasted

24 sheets phyllo dough, cut in half then covered with a slightly dampened cloth or plastic wrap

½ cup melted butter

Continues...

In a large frying pan on medium, heat oil then sauté lamb and onions for 10 minutes. Add garlic, cilantro, salt, black pepper, cumin, allspice, cinnamon, and Aleppo pepper, then sauté for 5 minutes. Transfer to a mixing bowl, then stir in peas, rice, and nuts. Divide into 12 portions and set aside.

Preheat oven to 350°F (180°C).

For each pie, brush 4 half-sheets of phyllo dough with butter and layer them on top of each other. Place a portion of filling in the middle, then fold the phyllo dough over the filling from all sides to make a square pie. Repeat until all 12 pies are done.

Place pies on a greased baking tray and brush with butter. Bake for 25 minutes or until pies are golden brown.

MAKES 12 PIES

Sittee Azbiqee

Lamb, Lentil, and Macaroni Medley

Once there was a woman whose grandparents bickered constantly. While she was helping her grandmother cook one day, her grandfather entered the kitchen. When the grandmother saw her husband, she ran and hid in a corner to avoid his argumentative mood. The grandfather had his head turned to look at what was on the stove and asked his granddaughter, "What are you cooking?" Before answering him, she whispered to her grandmother, "*Sittee, zb'ee!*" "Quick, Grandmother, get out!" And her grandfather assumed this was the name of the dish. Another story is that *azbiqee* refers to the metal mercury because despite being hearty and filling, this dish is eaten as easily as mercury flows.

¾ cup (150 g) brown lentils

¾ cup (75 g) elbow macaroni

1¾ tsp salt, divided

1 tbsp olive oil

5 garlic cloves, crushed

½ cup (25 g) finely chopped cilantro

4 tbsp butter, divided

1 small onion, finely chopped

½ lb (250 g) ground lamb

1¼ tsp black pepper, divided

1 tsp *baharaat*

½ tsp allspice

1 tbsp *dibs rummaan*

2 cups (500 mL) boiling water

1½ tsp cumin

1½ tsp coriander

2 tbsp lemon juice

1 large onion, thinly sliced and deep-fried until golden

1 cup (35 g) toasted Arab bread pieces

1 large lemon, cut in wedges (optional)

Continues...

Rinse lentils, cook for 12 to 15 minutes in a pot of water, then drain well.

Cook macaroni in another pot of water with ½ tsp salt for 6 minutes, then drain well.

In a frying pan on medium, heat oil and sauté garlic for 2 minutes, then add cilantro and sauté for 2 minutes. Set aside.

In a deep saucepan on medium heat, melt 2 tbsp butter and sauté finely chopped onions until soft, 8 minutes. Stir in lamb and cook for 5 minutes. Add ½ tsp salt, ½ tsp pepper, *baharaat,* allspice, and *dibs rummaan.* Stir and cook for 3 minutes.

Add boiling water to meat, then add lentils, remaining salt and pepper, cumin, coriander, lemon juice, and remaining butter. Gently stir and cook on medium heat for 10 minutes, then stir in macaroni and garlic-cilantro mixture and cook for 5 minutes.

Transfer to a platter and serve immediately, garnished with deep-fried onions, toasted Arab bread and a lemon wedge per person, if desired.

MAKES 6 SERVINGS

The traditional recipe, some say more than 200 years old, calls for small pieces of dough. Today, macaroni is used to save time.

Mufarrika

Syrian Scramble

Until a few generations ago, this dish was made with *qawarma* (see p. 62) instead of ground meat. Today, vegetable oil or butter replaces the fat that originally came from the *qawarma*.

There's a saying in Arabic: "*Illii maaluu qadiim maaluu jadiid*" ("He who has nothing old has nothing new"). These words aptly describe *mufarrika*, a dish that has stood the test of time because it's one of those simple yet tasty meals that can be whipped together last minute. *Mufarraka* means "to cut in equal pieces," which refers to the cubed potato. Cooks will be happy to know this is the most difficult part of the preparation. *Kousa* (squash or zucchini) may be substituted for the potatoes.

4 tbsp butter, divided
1 lb (500 g) ground lamb or beef
¾ tsp salt
½ tsp black pepper
½ tsp *baharaat*
pinch Aleppo pepper
½ cup (125 mL) vegetable oil
1 large onion, finely chopped

5 cups ½-in (1-cm) potato cubes (peel removed), sprinkled with salt
5 eggs, beaten
a few sprigs of parsley
3 tbsp finely chopped green onions

In a frying pan on medium heat, melt 2 tbsp butter and sauté meat for 10 minutes or until no longer pink. Add salt, pepper, *baharaat,* and Aleppo pepper and cook for 5 minutes, stirring frequently. Set aside and keep warm.

In a saucepan on medium, heat oil and sauté onions until soft, about 8 minutes. Stir in potatoes. Adjust seasoning. Stir, reduce heat to medium-low, cover, and cook for 30 minutes, or until potatoes are tender, stirring frequently

Continues...

to keep from sticking to pan. Stir in remaining butter until melted, then add cooked meat. Stir and cook for 1 minute.

Gently stir in eggs and cook for 2 to 3 minutes, or until the eggs are set.

Transfer to a serving dish, garnish with parsley and green onions, and serve hot.

MAKES 6 TO 8 SERVINGS

Zunoud al-Banaat

Syrian Scotch Egg

We enjoyed this dish in Damascus, accompanied with fried potatoes and a tomato salad.

1 lb (500 g) ground lamb or beef

1 medium onion, chopped

1 cup (25 g) chopped fresh
   parsley

1 tsp salt

1 tsp cumin

½ tsp black pepper

¼ tsp allspice

⅛ tsp Aleppo pepper

4 hard-boiled eggs, peeled

1 cup (250 mL) stewed tomatoes, pureed

1 cup (250 mL) water

Preheat oven to 350°F (180°C).

In a food processor, combine all ingredients except eggs, tomatoes, and water into a thick paste. Divide into 4 balls, then flatten into rounds. Place an egg in the middle of each round and wrap meat around the egg to form a ball. Place balls in a casserole dish, then pour tomatoes and water over them. Bake uncovered for 40 minutes or until meat is no longer pink inside.

Remove from oven and let stand for 15 minutes, then slice balls into ¼-in (6-mm) thick slices. Place on a serving platter, spread sauce over top, and serve.

MAKES 6 SERVINGS

Al-Baatrush al-Hamawee

The Union of Eggplant and Seasoned Meat

A unique variation of the more common baba ganoush, *al-baatrush al-hamawee* is a beloved specialty of the city of Hama. It is also called *mutabbal*, which translates to "spiced," "seasoned," or "flavored"—a perfect description of this exquisite dish.

This traditional recipe includes tahini and yogurt, whereas modern versions use tahini alone.

1 1-lb (500-g) eggplant

3 garlic cloves, minced

4 tbsp yogurt

½ tsp salt

2 tbsp tahini

2 tbsp lemon juice

1 tbsp olive oil

½ lb (250 g) lean ground lamb or beef

½ tsp salt

¼ tsp black pepper

¼ tsp *baharaat*

pinch Aleppo pepper

1 tsp *dibs rummaan*

½ cup (100 g) finely diced tomato

3 tbsp tomato paste diluted in ½ cup (125 mL) hot water

½ cup (65 g) coarsely chopped walnuts

¼ cup (5 g) finely chopped parsley

Preheat oven to 450°F (230°C).

Slit eggplant on each side and roast for 30 minutes, or until skin is crispy and flesh is very soft. Remove from oven and allow to cool until it is not too hot to touch. Scoop out flesh, discard skin and stem, and place flesh in a strainer. Allow excess water to drain for 15 minutes.

In a mixing bowl, mash together eggplant and garlic. Add yogurt, salt, tahini, and lemon juice. Mash together and spread on a serving platter.

In a frying pan on medium, heat oil and sauté meat, stirring constantly, until brown, 10 to 12 minutes. Add salt, black pepper, *baharaat*, Aleppo pepper, and *dibs rummaan* and sauté for 2 minutes. Add tomatoes and sauté for 3 minutes. Stir in diluted tomato paste, reduce heat to low, and cook for 15 minutes, stirring occasionally.

Spoon meat mixture over eggplant mixture, top with walnuts, and garnish with parsley.

MAKES 6 SERVINGS

Shaykh al-Mihshee
Meat and Eggplant Casserole

Shaykh means "leader" or "chief," and *shaykh al-mihshee* is, indeed, the leader of all stuffed vegetables. It can be prepared with eggplant or *kousa* (squash or zucchini) and cooked in either yogurt or tomato sauce. Small eggplants can be stuffed with meat and pine nuts, or large ones can be layered to form a casserole. Serve hot over *ruzz mufalfal* (p. 54) or *ruzz bi-sha'eereeya* (p. 55) to soak up the sauce.

¾ tsp salt

3 lb (1.5 kg) eggplant, sliced in
  ½-in (1-cm) rounds

vegetable oil for deep-frying

2 cups (400 g) *kubba* stuffing
  (p.168)

1 6-oz (178-mL) can tomato paste

4½ cups (1.1 L) boiling water

½ tsp black pepper

Lightly salt eggplant slices and let sit for at least 6 to 8 hours or overnight in a colander to drain.

Shake eggplant of any excess water. In a frying pan on medium-high, heat oil and deep-fry eggplant until golden on both sides. Remove and drain on paper towels.

Preheat oven to 350°F (180°C).

Layer half the eggplant in a 9 x 13-in (3.5-L) casserole dish. Spread stuffing evenly over the top, then cover with remaining eggplant.

In a mixing bowl, combine remaining ingredients and pour over the casserole. Cover and bake for 1 hour.

MAKES 6 TO 8 SERVINGS

Fattat Makdous

Eggplant and Ground Meat Fatteh

Fatteh dishes use toasted Arab bread as the base upon which to showcase other ingredients, such as chickpeas, chicken, and the most popular in Damascus—eggplant.

16 baby eggplants, 1–1½ in (2.5–4 cm) long

1 cup (250 mL) *labna*

4 tbsp tahini

2 tbsp *dibs rummaan*

4 garlic cloves, crushed

1½ tsp salt, divided

4 tbsp butter

2 tbsp pine nuts

4 tbsp coarsely ground walnuts

4 tbsp olive oil

1 lb (500 g) lean ground beef

1 tsp black pepper

vegetable oil for deep-frying

6 small loaves of Arab bread, split open, cut into 1½-in (4-cm) pieces, and toasted

8 tbsp tomato paste diluted in 3 cups (700 mL) water

1 cup (250 mL) yogurt

4 tbsp finely chopped parsley

Rinse eggplants well, remove stems, and slice off tops. Peel eggplants, leaving some strips of peel so that they are striped. Rinse eggplants, then sprinkle salt lightly all over them. Set aside.

For the sauce: In a bowl, mix together *labna*, tahini, *dibs rummaan*, garlic, and ½ tsp salt. Set aside.

In a frying pan on medium-low heat, melt butter and sauté pine nuts until golden, 3 to 4 minutes. Remove pine nuts with a slotted spoon, leaving the butter in the pan, and drain on paper towel.

Continues…

In the same frying pan, sauté walnuts until golden, 3 to 4 minutes. Remove walnuts with slotted spoon and drain on paper towel.

For the stuffing: In a frying pan on medium, heat oil and sauté beef until cooked through, about 10 minutes. Stir in remaining 1 tsp salt, pepper, pine nuts, and walnuts. Set aside.

In a saucepan on medium, deep-fry eggplants in enough vegetable oil to cover them by ½ in (1 cm) until they begin to brown, about 5 to 8 minutes. Drain on paper towels. Let cool for 5 minutes. With a knife, slit each eggplant vertically down the middle to create a pocket, making sure to not cut right through. Stuff eggplants with beef mixture and gently close the opening. Set aside to cool.

On a serving platter, evenly spread the toasted bread pieces and set aside.

In a bowl, mix the sauce with the diluted tomato paste. In a saucepan on medium heat, bring mixture to a soft boil, stirring occasionally.

Pour hot sauce over bread pieces, then spoon yogurt over top. Carefully place stuffed eggplants on top, then sprinkle parsley.

Serve immediately.

MAKES 8 SERVINGS

Maariyaa

Spicy Grilled Lamb Sandwich

Crisp on the outside and moist and tender on the inside, these sandwich triangles are eaten right off the grill in Damascus. Natives of
Deir ez-Zor call their version *maareenaa*, claiming it's named after the
woman who created it, thus setting the gold standard: garlic is part
of the meat mixture, and the sandwich is turned whole in a grate on
the grill, over and over until it is browned and ready to eat. Preparing
them is a family affair, with everyone sitting outside around the grill,
grabbing a piece before the dish hits the table. But *maariyaa* is so tasty
that no one, in Deir ez-Zor or anywhere, is satisfied with just one.
Serve this with lemon slices and fresh or pickled vegetables or salad.

1 lb (500 g) ground lamb

1 medium onion, chopped

1 medium tomato, skin removed
   and chopped

½ cup (90 g) chopped green bell
   pepper

½ cup (90 g) chopped red bell
   pepper

1 cup (25 g) chopped parsley

1 tsp finely chopped jalapeño

4 tbsp fresh mint, or 2 tsp dried
   mint, crushed

1 tsp salt

½ tsp black pepper

1 tsp *baharaat*

½ tsp allspice

¼ tsp cinnamon

2 tbsp *dibs rummaan*

2 large loaves Arab bread

3 tbsp olive oil

sumac for sprinkling (optional)

Preheat oven to 350°F (180°C).

In a food processor, blend all ingredients except bread and oil for 2 minutes.

Cut 1 loaf of Arab bread in four triangles. Open each triangle by carefully separating the top from the bottom. Pat some meat mixture into each triangle and then press to close. Repeat with the other loaf. Brush oil on both sides of triangles, place on a baking tray, and bake for 25 minutes.

Transfer to a platter and sprinkle with sumac, if desired.

MAKES 8 SANDWICHES

Chicken & Fish

Salloum's Spicy Fried Chicken

This is fried chicken Syrian style, with the unique aromatic tang of za'atar. Serve with *sals al-thoum* (see p. 64) and lemon wedges.

6 chicken drumsticks, fat and excess skin trimmed

6 boneless chicken thighs, fat and excess skin trimmed

1 tsp salt

1 tsp black pepper

1 tsp allspice

2 tbsp za'atar

6 garlic cloves, crushed

¼ tsp Aleppo pepper

2 eggs, beaten

4 tbsp water

2 cups (300 g) white flour

vegetable oil for deep-frying

In a large mixing bowl, toss chicken with salt, black pepper, allspice, za'atar, garlic, Aleppo pepper, eggs, and water. Mix well until chicken is fully coated. Cover with plastic wrap and refrigerate overnight.

Dredge chicken in flour, coating all pieces well. Spread chicken pieces on flat surface.

In a large frying pan on medium, heat 1 in (2.5 cm) oil. Add a few chicken pieces, making sure they do not touch. Cover and cook for 7 minutes. Turn chicken, cover, and cook for 7 minutes. Remove cover, increase heat to medium-high, and cook for 5 minutes, turning frequently to ensure all sides are golden. Remove chicken and drain on paper towel. Continue until all pieces are fried.

MAKES 6 SERVINGS

Dajaaj ma'a Thoum

Chicken with Garlic

In the 18th and 19th centuries, Syrian families raised chickens for their eggs, not only in the rural areas but also in Damascus. Eggs were a daily breakfast food and a source of income. Only the wealthy ate meat or chicken every day. For others, these foods were reserved for holidays and celebrations.

12 chicken drumsticks (about 3 lb [1.5 kg])	½ head garlic, crushed
1 tsp white vinegar	¼ tsp black pepper
1½ tsp salt, divided	1 cup (250 mL) lemon juice
	½ cup (125 mL) olive oil

Score each drumstick about ½ in (1 cm), then place in a bowl and cover with 1 in (2.5 cm) cold water. Stir in vinegar and ½ tsp salt, then refrigerate for 1 hour. Drain drumsticks, rinse, and transfer to a deep bowl.

In another bowl, mix remaining salt, garlic, pepper, lemon juice, and oil. Pour over drumsticks and mix well. Cover and refrigerate for 30 minutes.

Preheat oven to 325°F (160°C).

Place drumsticks side by side in a casserole dish, then pour marinade over them. Cover and bake for 2½ hours, basting every 30 minutes. Chicken should be very tender and falling off the bone.

Remove cover and broil for 2 to 3 minutes or until the top of the chicken browns. For best results, baste chicken once or twice while broiling.

MAKES 4 TO 6 SERVINGS

Dajaaj ma'a Ruzz

Chicken and Rice

Arab hospitality dictates that the best is laid out on the table when guests arrive. In Syria, this means *dajaaj ma'a ruzz*, a spectacular rice dish richly decorated with toasted almonds and pine nuts, a welcome sight for hungry eyes.

2 unsplit bone-in chicken breasts, fat trimmed and skin removed

1 onion, quartered

¾ tsp black pepper, divided

2 3-in (8-cm) cinnamon sticks

½ tsp cinnamon powder, divided

¾ tsp allspice, divided

½ tsp coriander, divided

⅛ tsp cayenne, divided

2 tbsp chicken broth powder

½ tsp salt, divided

3 tbsp butter

1 lb (500 g) sirloin steak, minced

¼ tsp garlic powder

2 cups (400 g) basmati or other long-grain white rice, soaked for 30 minutes then drained

½ cup (70 g) pine nuts, toasted in butter

1 cup (110 g) sliced or slivered almonds, toasted in butter

In a large saucepan, cover chicken with 2 to 3 in (5 to 8 cm) water. Add onion, ½ tsp pepper, cinnamon sticks, ¼ tsp cinnamon, ½ tsp allspice, ¼ tsp coriander, pinch of cayenne, and chicken broth powder, stir, and bring to a boil. Let boil for 5 minutes, skimming to remove froth.

Reduce heat to medium-low, cover, and cook for 1 hour, or until meat pulls easily from the bone, stirring occasionally. Check seasoning before adding

¼ tsp salt, because broth powder usually contains salt. Strain contents and reserve broth. Set aside.

Remove chicken from strainer and discard bones. Then shred chicken, return to reserved broth, and keep warm.

In a frying pan on medium heat, melt butter and sauté beef for 2 minutes. Add garlic powder and remaining salt, pepper, cinnamon, allspice, coriander, and cayenne. Stir and cook for 5 minutes. Set aside.

Strain chicken, reserving 3¼ cups (770 mL) broth.

In a large saucepan, place 3 cups (700 mL) reserved broth, cooked beef, and rice. Stir well and bring to a boil. Reduce heat to low, cover, and cook for 12 to 15 minutes, stirring occasionally to ensure rice doesn't stick. (If rice is not cooked yet, add a little extra broth, cover, and continue cooking for another 2 minutes.) Remove from heat and let sit for 10 minutes.

Transfer rice to a serving platter, spread chicken over top, then garnish with nuts.

MAKES 6 TO 8 SERVINGS

Freekat al-Dajaaj

Freekeh with Chicken

Habeeb's parents grew wheat on their homestead from which they made freekeh. The rare year they had a crop in that arid part of Canada, Shams would cut the wheat when it began to turn yellow and the seeds were still soft, and then spread it in the sun to dry. When the wheat was bone dry, it was carefully set on fire so that the straw burned but not the seeds. Next came the stage that gave the grain its name—the children helped rub (*faraka* in Arabic) the roasted wheat to remove the chaff. Again, the seeds were left in the sun to dry, and the kernels were coarsely ground. Our love of freekeh has traveled down the generations, and now our family and friends freak out for freekeh—because it's so freaking good!

Freekeh

2 lb (900 g) bone-in chicken breasts, skin removed and fat trimmed

2 3-in (8-cm) cinnamon sticks

2 tsp salt

1 tsp black pepper

1 medium onion, quartered

½ tsp allspice

1 tsp *baharaat*

¼ tsp Aleppo pepper

6 tbsp butter

2 cups (450 g) freekeh, washed twice and drained

4 tbsp pine nuts, toasted

In a saucepan, cover chicken with water, then add cinnamon sticks, salt, black pepper, onion, allspice, *baharaat,* and Aleppo pepper. Bring to a boil, skim to remove froth, reduce heat to medium-low, cover, and cook for 1 hour or until chicken pulls easily from the bone.

Remove chicken pieces with a slotted spoon and debone, reserving broth. With a fork, shred meat. Set aside.

Strain broth and reserve 4 cups (1 L).

In a saucepan on medium heat, melt butter and sauté freekeh and for 3 minutes. Stir in reserved broth, add chicken, and bring to a boil. Reduce heat to medium-low, cover, and cook for 25 minutes, stirring occasionally to ensure freekeh does not stick. Remove from heat and let sit for 20 minutes.

Transfer to a platter, decorate with pine nuts, and serve immediately.

MAKES 6 SERVINGS

Maghrabeeya

Chicken and Pearl Couscous

Maghrabeeya looks like large beads and is sold as *moghrabieh* or pearl couscous. *Maghrabeeya* means "of Morocco," the region where cous-cous originated. In Greater Syria, *maghrabeeya* was originally made by hand, by gradually adding flour to a little bulgur to make small balls.

2 lb (900 g) chicken pieces, any cut

2 tsp salt, divided

⅛ tsp *baharaat*

4 tbsp olive oil

2 cinnamon sticks

2 bay leaves

¼ tsp ground cloves

1 tsp black pepper, divided

2 cups small onions such as pearl or boiling, peeled

1 19-oz (540-mL) can chickpeas, drained and rinsed

3 cups (700 mL) water

2 cups (340 g) pearl couscous

4 tbsp butter

1 cup (250 mL) hot chicken broth

Spice mix

2 tsp caraway seeds

¼ tsp cinnamon

1 tsp *baharaat*

1 tsp cumin

Wash chicken with a little vinegar and water, pat dry, and sprinkle with 1 tsp salt and *baharaat.*

In a deep saucepan on medium, heat oil, place chicken pieces skin side down, and brown on one side until skin is crispy, about 5 minutes, then flip over to brown and crisp the other side.

Cover chicken with 2 in (5 cm) water, then add cinnamon sticks, bay leaves, cloves, ½ tsp salt, and ½ tsp pepper. Bring to a boil and skim to remove froth and fat. Reduce heat to medium, cover, and cook for 45 minutes, stirring occasionally.

Add onion, cover, and cook for 10 minutes. Remove cinnamon sticks and bay leaves.

Stir in chickpeas, three-quarters of the spice mix, and remaining salt and pepper. Reduce heat to medium-low, cover, and simmer for 15 minutes. Set aside.

In another saucepan, bring 3 cups (700 mL) water to a boil and add couscous. Reduce heat to medium-low, and cook until tender, 15 to 20 minutes. Drain couscous.

In a saucepan on medium-low heat, melt butter and stir together pearl couscous and remaining spice mix for 2 minutes. Add 1 cup (250 mL) hot chicken broth from the saucepan that had been set aside, reduce heat to low, and simmer for 10 minutes, stirring occasionally.

Ladle couscous into bowls, top with chicken, and then spoon remaining saucepan broth with onions and chickpeas over top. Serve hot.

MAKES 6 SERVINGS

Dajaaj ma'a Hummus

Chicken with Chickpeas

In the 18th and 19th centuries, *hummus* vendors in the souks of Damascus peddled their hot chickpea dishes, especially in winter. Serve this with *ruzz mufalfal* (see p. 54).

4 tbsp butter

3–5 lb (1.5–2.2 kg) whole chicken, trimmed of fat and cut into 8 pieces

2 medium onions, finely chopped

4 garlic cloves, crushed

¼ cup (15 g) finely chopped cilantro

1 19-oz (540-mL) can chickpeas, drained

2 cups (500 mL) water

3 tbsp tomato paste, dissolved in 1 cup (250 mL) water

2 tsp salt

1 tsp *baharaat*

1 tsp black pepper

¼ tsp chili powder

In a saucepan on medium heat, melt butter then sauté chicken pieces, turning several times to brown evenly. Remove chicken and set aside.

In the same saucepan on medium heat, sauté onions for 8 minutes or until they begin to brown. Add garlic and cilantro and sauté for 3 minutes. Stir in chicken and remaining ingredients and bring to a boil. Reduce heat to medium, cover, and simmer for 30 minutes, stirring occasionally, until meat can be pulled from the bone easily. Serve hot.

MAKES 6 TO 8 SERVINGS

Dajaaj ma'a Burghul wa Banadoura

Chicken with Bulgur and Tomatoes

This dish is an easy and tasty way to use up leftover cooked chicken.

6 tbsp olive oil

4 medium onions, finely chopped

4 garlic cloves, minced

½ jalapeño, seeded and very finely chopped

1½ cups (150 g) finely chopped green onions

2 cups (450 g) coarse (#3 or #4) bulgur, rinsed and drained

4 medium tomatoes, finely chopped

1¾ tsp salt

1 tsp black pepper

½ tsp *baharaat*

2¼ cups (530 mL) water

2 tbsp butter

3 cups (375 g) shredded cooked chicken, warmed

In a deep saucepan on medium, heat oil and sauté onion until soft and golden, about 8 minutes. Add garlic and jalapeño and sauté for 3 minutes. Add green onions and sauté for 3 minutes. Stir in bulgur, mix well, and sauté for 1 minute. Stir in tomatoes. Cover, reduce heat to medium-low, and cook for 10 minutes, stirring frequently.

Stir in spices and water. Mix well and bring to a boil. Reduce heat to low, cover, and simmer for 20 to 25 minutes, or until bulgur is soft and liquid is absorbed, stirring occasionally. Stir in butter. Remove from heat, cover, and let sit for 10 minutes. Place in a serving dish and spread chicken over top. Serve with yogurt.

MAKES 8 SERVINGS

Dajaaj ma'a Dibs Rummaan

Chicken with Pomegranate Molasses

Three types of pomegranate were cultivated in the 18th century in Syria— sweet, sour, and a variety that was sweet and sour. They were abundant in Aleppo's gardens, described as thickets of natural wonder, especially after August. They would be dried or made into molasses, to be enjoyed through winter. Serve this over a bed of rice.

4 tbsp olive oil

3 lb (1.5 kg) whole chicken, cut into 8 pieces

1 tsp paprika

1 tsp *baharaat*

1 tsp salt

1 tsp black pepper

2 medium onions, finely chopped

4 garlic cloves, crushed

4 tbsp finely chopped cilantro

½ small jalapeño, seeded and minced

3 tbsp *dibs rummaan*

2 cups (500 mL) stewed tomatoes, pureed

3 cups (700 mL) water

In a saucepan on medium-high, heat oil then add chicken and sprinkle with paprika, *baharaat,* salt, and pepper. Sauté for 5 minutes, turning once, then stir in remaining ingredients and bring to a boil. Reduce heat to medium, cover, and cook for 45 minutes or until chicken is tender, stirring occasionally.

MAKES 6 TO 8 SERVINGS

Dajaaj Mihshee bil-Burghul

Chicken with Bulgur Stuffing

Syrians have their own style of bulgur stuffing for chicken. It is more common outside the major cities and represents the genius of creativity among those who cannot afford the luxuries of meat and rice every day.

1 large roasting chicken, about 4–5 lb (1.8–2.2 kg)

½ cup (113 g) butter

½ cup (70 g) pine nuts

½ cup (75 g) finely chopped onion

1 cup (225 g) coarse (#3 or #4) bulgur, soaked in hot water for 5 minutes then drained

1 cup (250 mL) chicken stock

¼ cup (5 g) finely chopped parsley

1½ tsp salt, divided

¾ tsp black pepper, divided

½ tsp allspice

1 tsp coriander

3 tbsp melted butter

1 tsp cinnamon

Wash and dry chicken, then set aside.

In a frying pan on medium-low heat, melt ½ cup (113 g) butter and sauté pine nuts until golden, then remove with a slotted spoon and set aside. Reserve butter in pan.

For the stuffing: In the same frying pan on medium-low heat, sauté onions in reserved butter for 10 minutes. Add bulgur and sauté for 2 minutes. Add chicken stock, parsley, ½ tsp salt, ¼ tsp pepper, allspice, and coriander. Stir occasionally until stock is absorbed, about 10 minutes. Remove from heat and allow to cool, then stir in pine nuts.

Preheat oven to 350°F (180°C).

Stuff chicken and sew closed with a trussing needle and cooking twine, then place in a roasting pan. Brush the chicken with 3 tbsp butter and sprinkle with remaining salt, pepper, and cinnamon. Cover and roast for 2 hours. Remove cover and roast for 30 minutes until chicken is golden.

Remove stuffing from chicken and transfer to a serving dish. Carve chicken and serve over stuffing.

MAKES 6 SERVINGS

Dajaaj Mihshee bil-Lahm wa Mukassaraat

Chicken Stuffed with Rice and Nuts

Mihshee means "stuffed," and this dish is not far from the elaborate *mihshees* of the 18th and 19th centuries, when mutton, rice, pistachios, pine nuts, almonds, currants, suet, spices, and garlic were a stuffing for vegetables and meat. However, such lavish ingredients were reserved for the tables of the upper classes.

Pistachios, walnuts, and pine nuts

1 large roasting chicken, about 5 lb (2.2 kg)

3 tbsp flour mixed with 1 tsp salt

¼ cup (60 mL) olive oil

½ lb (250 g) ground beef

1 medium onion, finely chopped

4 tbsp slivered almonds

4 tbsp whole raw cashews

4 tbsp pine nuts

½ cup (100 g) basmati or other long-grain white rice, rinsed and drained

4 tbsp raisins, soaked for 30 minutes then drained

½ tsp salt

1 tsp cinnamon, divided

1 tsp black pepper, divided

½ tsp cardamom, divided

½ tsp cloves, divided

1½ cups (375 mL) water

½ tsp dried rosemary

½ tsp dried sage

4 tbsp butter, at room temperature

Wash and dry chicken, then rub with the flour-salt mixture, both inside and out, and set aside.

For the stuffing: In a saucepan on medium-low, heat oil and sauté beef for 8 minutes. Add onions and sauté for 5 minutes. Stir in almonds, cashews, and pine nuts, then sauté for 3 minutes. Stir in rice, raisins, salt, ½ tsp cinnamon, ½ tsp pepper, ¼ tsp cardamom, ¼ tsp cloves, and 1 cup (250 mL) water. Bring to a boil, reduce heat to medium-low, and cook for 10 minutes, stirring a few times, then allow to cool.

For the basting sauce: In a small bowl, combine remaining cinnamon, pepper, cardamom, and cloves with rosemary, sage, and remaining water. Set aside.

Preheat oven to 375°F (190°C).

Stuff chicken, including neck opening. Sew closed and rub butter all over, then brush with some basting sauce. In a roasting pan, cover and roast for 1½ hours or until drumstick loosens when pulled, basting every 30 minutes.

Remove stuffing from chicken and transfer to a serving dish. Carve chicken and serve over stuffing.

MAKES 6 SERVINGS

Kubbat Samak

Fish Kibbeh

The best *kubbat samak* in Syria comes from the ancient island of Arwad, where saffron or paprika gives it a touch of color and it's stuffed with pine nuts and raisins. The best dipping sauce for these fish patties is *taratour* (see p. 67).

1 cup (225 g) fine (#1) bulgur

1 lb (500 g) cod or similar firm white fish fillet, cut into medium pieces

1 medium onion, chopped

4 garlic cloves, minced

4 tbsp flour

1½ tsp salt

1 tsp black pepper

½ tsp allspice

½ tsp cinnamon

¼ tsp nutmeg

⅛ tsp cayenne

oil for frying

Soak bulgur in warm water for 15 minutes, then press water out through a fine mesh strainer.

In a food processor, mix all ingredients except oil until it has the consistency of firm dough, adding more flour if necessary. Form into 1½-in (4-cm) patties.

In a frying pan on medium, heat 1 in (2.5 cm) oil, then fry patties, turning once, until golden brown. Drain on paper towels.

MAKES 6 TO 8 SERVINGS

Sayyadeeya

Syrian Fish Pilaf

This is a traditional recipe made throughout Syria and other Arab countries, usually served with *taratour* (see p. 67).

1 lb (500 g) fish fillets, any kind but preferably firm flesh, cut into 3-in (8-cm) pieces

½ tsp black pepper

½ tsp cumin

4 tbsp butter

1 large onion, finely chopped

2 garlic cloves, minced

½ cup (70 g) pine nuts

1 cup (200 g) basmati or other long-grain white rice, rinsed

1 tsp salt

⅛ tsp Aleppo pepper

2 cups (500 mL) water

1 large onion, thinly sliced and deep-fried

Sprinkle fish with pepper and cumin, then set aside.

In a frying pan on medium heat, melt butter and sauté fish for 6 minutes, turning once. Remove fish with a slotted spoon and set aside.

Preheat oven to 350°F (180°C).

In the same pan on medium-low heat, adding more butter if necessary, sauté onions, garlic, and pine nuts for 10 minutes. Add rice and sauté for 1 minute. Stir in salt, Aleppo pepper, and water and bring to a boil. Transfer to a greased casserole dish and arrange fish evenly on top.

Cover and bake for 30 minutes. Remove cover and bake for 10 minutes, or until rice is tender.

Garnish with deep-fried onions and serve immediately.

MAKES 4 TO 6 SERVINGS

Samak bil-Taheena

Baked Fish with Tahini Sauce

In Greater Syria, baked fish is always served with tahini sauce.

olive oil for brushing

2 lb (900 g) firm white fish
　　fillets

salt and pepper

1 lemon, thinly sliced

juice of 1 lemon

1 tsp sumac

4 tbsp pine nuts + 4 tbsp split
　　almonds, toasted in 2 tbsp
　　butter

2 tbsp finely chopped parsley

2 tbsp finely chopped cilantro

Tahini sauce

¾ cup tahini

½ cup (125 mL) lemon juice

½ cup (125 mL) water

4 garlic cloves, crushed

¾ tsp salt

½ tsp pepper

Preheat oven to 375°F (190°C).

Place a sheet of tinfoil in a baking pan and brush lightly with oil. Place fish
fillets on top and sprinkle with salt and pepper. Evenly spread lemon slices
over fillets and sprinkle lemon juice, then dust sumac evenly over top. Cover
with tinfoil and bake for 20 to 25 minutes, or until fish flakes easily with a fork.

While fish is baking, in a bowl, whisk together tahini sauce ingredients and
set aside.

When fish is cooked, carefully remove from foil and place on a serving
platter. Drizzle tahini sauce over each fillet. Sprinkle with toasted nuts and
garnish with parsley and cilantro. Serve immediately.

MAKES 8 SERVINGS

Samak Mishwee

Baked Whole Fish

Habeeb first tasted this version of *samak mishwee* in Damascus in the 1960s, at the home of a friend who had invited him for a special meal. When Habeeb told his host he had never had a simple dish that tasted so good, Fu'ad replied, "In Damascus, we've been eating this for centuries—not the same fish, but rather, how we make it!" Serve this with *taratour* (see p. 67) and lemon slices.

2 whole red snapper, about 1 lb (500 g) each, scaled and gutted

olive oil for brushing
salt and pepper

Clean the fish, lightly salt inside and out, and refrigerate on a tray for 2 hours.

Preheat oven to 400°F (200°C).

Rinse fish and pat dry. Place each fish on a lightly greased sheet of tinfoil big enough to wrap around it. Brush fish with oil, then sprinkle inside and out with salt and pepper. Wrap in foil and bake for 30 to 35 minutes, or until fish flakes easily with a fork. Unwrap and broil for 5 minutes or until skin is lightly browned.

MAKES 2 SERVINGS

Samak Harra

Spicy Stuffed Whole Fish

This showstopper of a dish is a whole fish, rubbed with spices, then stuffed and taken to the table straight out of the oven. Make sure to have a batch of *taratour* (see p. 67) ready to drizzle over each serving.

3–4 lb (1.5–1.8 kg) whole salmon or red snapper, cleaned

2½ tsp salt, divided

1 tsp cumin

1 tsp black pepper

1 tsp *baharaat*

2 cups (100 g) finely chopped cilantro

8 garlic cloves, crushed

2 medium carrots, grated

1 large red bell pepper, seeded and julienned

1 tbsp finely chopped, seeded jalapeño

1 tbsp *dibs rummaan*

2 tbsp olive oil

Cut slits ½ to 1 in (1 to 2.5 cm) long into fish's skin, then rub fish inside and out with 2 tsp salt, cumin, black pepper, and *baharaat*.

In a bowl, combine cilantro, garlic, carrots, bell pepper, jalapeño, *dibs rummaan*, and remaining ½ tsp salt. Stuff fish and close with toothpicks. Brush fish all over with olive oil, then wrap with tinfoil. Refrigerate for 4 hours.

Preheat oven to 350°F (180°C).

Place wrapped fish on a baking tray and bake for 40 minutes. Remove from oven and uncover the top of the fish. Bake uncovered for 10 minutes.

Transfer to a serving platter and carefully unwrap.

MAKES 6 SERVINGS

Samak Miqlee

Whole Fried Fish

One of the most memorable meals our family ever had was in a small restaurant in Deir ez-Zor, on the edge of the Euphrates. In the true tradition of Arab hospitality, the proprietor would not let us leave, insisting we had not visited Deir ez-Zor until we had tasted the fish that was prepared there. We sat with his family and enjoyed a dish of fried fish that, until this day, has yet to meet its match. He told us it was the breezes from Iraq that added to its flavor.

4 tbsp olive oil

1 tbsp sumac

1 tsp salt

½ tsp cumin

½ tsp coriander

½ tsp black pepper

½ tsp ground ginger

⅛ tsp cayenne

½ tsp turmeric

⅛ tsp cinnamon

6 garlic cloves, crushed

1 lemon, chopped

2 lb (900 g) whole snapper, scaled, cleaned inside and out, and patted dry

vegetable oil for deep-frying

In a small bowl, combine oil, sumac, salt, cumin, coriander, pepper, ginger, cayenne, turmeric, and cinnamon.

In another small bowl, combine garlic and lemon, then stuff fish with this mixture.

Brush outside of fish on both sides with the oil and spice mixture. Cover and refrigerate overnight.

In a nonstick frying pan on medium heat, add vegetable oil to cover at least

2 in (5 cm) above fish. Deep-fry fish for 4 minutes on one side, turn, and fry for another 4 minutes until fish is golden.

Serve immediately.

MAKES 2 SERVINGS

Vegetables

Foul Mudammas

Fava Bean Potage

Foul mudammas is associated with Egypt more than any other Arab country, where it is served for breakfast. Syrians continue the tradition; however, they have one-upped this filling dish with the addition of chickpeas. There is nothing more satisfying than a bowl of *foul mudammas* served with a variety of fresh vegetables and scooped up with Arab bread. Leila's children are so gung ho about a breakfast of *foul mudammas* with all its trimmings that they will drive in the early morning to make sure they are there as the first scoop comes out of the pot. Yes, Syrian genes are strong.

We use canned fava beans and chickpeas simply because they take less time to prepare. But we opt for the good ol' way of crushing garlic with a pestle. The signature Syrian marriage of new and old, modern and traditional.

5 garlic cloves

¼ cup (60 mL) lemon juice

¼ cup (60 mL) olive oil

½ tsp salt

¼ tsp black pepper

¾ tsp cumin

2 19-oz (540-mL) cans plain fava beans, undrained

1 19-oz (540-mL) can chickpeas, undrained

1 bunch parsley, finely chopped

1 large tomato, finely chopped

2 tsp sumac

1 small bunch green onions

1 lemon, cut in wedges

1 large onion, quartered

Arab bread

In a serving bowl, crush garlic with a pestle, then stir in lemon juice, oil, salt, pepper, and cumin. Set aside.

In a saucepan on medium-high heat, bring fava beans and chickpeas with their liquid to a boil, stirring occasionally. Reduce heat to medium-low, cover,

Continues…

and cook for 10 minutes, stirring occasionally.

Remove from heat and ladle hot beans into the serving bowl with ¼ cup (60 mL) of the saucepan liquid. With the pestle used to crush the garlic or a heavy wooden spoon, crush some of the beans.

Garnish with some parsley and tomatoes. Serve in individual bowls with additional parsley, tomatoes, sumac, green onions and a squeeze of lemon. Use Arab bread or quartered onions to scoop up.

MAKES 4 TO 6 SERVINGS

Taqlaayat al-Foul

Stir-Fried Fresh Fava Beans

In the mid-18th and early 19th centuries, fava beans were one of the major crops planted in the fields around Aleppo and were in season from April to July. Simple to prepare, this Damascene dish is a refreshing vegetarian side or entrée. Serve with *khiyaar bil-laban* (see p. 140) or *lift* (see p. 89).

½ cup (125 mL) olive oil, divided

2 lb (900 g) fresh fava beans

1 cup (250 mL) water, divided

2 heads garlic, peeled and
   crushed

1 tsp salt

2 cups (100 g) finely chopped
   cilantro

lemon wedges (optional)

Arab bread

In a saucepan on medium-high, heat ¼ cup (60 mL) oil and sauté fava beans for 2 minutes. Add ¾ cup (175 mL) water and bring to a boil, reduce heat to medium, cover, and cook until beans are tender, about 15 minutes, stirring occasionally. Add remaining ¼ cup (60 mL) water, cover, and cook for 2 minutes. Stir in garlic and salt and cook for 2 minutes. Remove from heat. Stir in cilantro and mix well, then stir in remaining oil.

Transfer to a serving platter. Serve hot or cold with a squeeze of lemon over each serving for some extra zest. Scoop up beans with Arab bread so that no part of the dish goes to waste.

MAKES 6 SERVINGS

Mujaddara

Lentil Potage

In the 18th, 19th, and even early 20th centuries, during their weekly visit to the centuries-old neighborhood public bathhouses for relaxation and full-body cleansing, Syrian women kept up with the latest gossip, jokes, and stories over a communal lunch of *mujaddara* with a side of pickled turnips. As it is today, this was their comfort food. When Syrians first began to emigrate in large numbers in response to Ottoman occupation, they brought *mujaddara* with them. The majority were peasants for whom *mujaddara* was a nutritious staple food. Ironically, over time, these same immigrants would be embarrassed to offer a guest this dish that cost pennies to make. In 1904, the *New York Times* said *mujaddara* was considered "very bourgeois," not finding a place on the tables of the wealthy, yet "an aristocrat is very fond of his mojaddara" and "will gladly partake of it in secret." Serve this with *lift* (see p. 89).

As for the name *mujaddara*, a rather morbid theory suggested by modern storytellers is that the white rice is supposed to represent a young, fair-skinned girl who becomes afflicted with *jadree*, smallpox.

1 cup (200 g) green or brown
    lentils, rinsed

6 cups (1.5 L) water

¼ cup (50 g) basmati or other
    long grain white rice, rinsed

4 tbsp butter

3 medium onions, finely
    chopped

1 tsp salt

1 tsp cumin

½ tsp black pepper

½ tsp coriander

Arab bread

In a saucepan, bring lentils and water to a boil, then reduce heat to medium, cover, and cook for 40 minutes. Add rice and cook for 15 minutes or until lentils and rice are tender, adding more water if necessary.

Meanwhile, in a frying pan on medium heat, melt butter and sauté onions for 10 minutes or until golden brown. Add frying pan contents and remaining ingredients to lentils, then cook for 5 minutes.

Serve hot with Arab bread for scooping.

MAKES 6 SERVINGS

Haraaq Usba'u

Lentils with Dumplings

Once there was a man who could not stay away from the kitchen when his wife was cooking. One day, he put his finger in the pot for a taste and immediately started to wave his hand around, yelling loudly in pain. At that moment, their son walked in and asked his mom, "Hey! What's cooking?" She assumed he was asking about what had happened and answered, "*Haraaq usba'u* (he burnt his finger)." The son thought this was what the dish was called and went to tell his siblings what they would be eating for dinner.

A dish unique to Damascus, haraaq usba'u is one of the city's most traditional and famous foods. Some consider it an appetizer, whereas for others it is their main meal. Traditionally, this was served as the farewell dish for a bride when she had her last meal at her parents' house with her sisters and girlfriends. It was also one of the seven dishes served during the seven-day celebrations after the wedding.

1 cup (200 g) green or brown lentils, rinsed
7 cups (1.75 L) water
½ lb (250 g) frozen bread dough, thawed
1 tsp salt
1 tsp black pepper
½ tsp cumin
⅛ tsp cayenne
3 tbsp lemon juice
4 tbsp olive oil
1 large onion, finely chopped
vegetable oil for deep-frying
½ cup (25 g) finely chopped cilantro
4 garlic cloves, crushed
seeds of 1 pomegranate

In a saucepan, bring lentils and water to a boil. Reduce heat to me-dium, cover, and cook for 30 minutes.

Meanwhile, roll dough ⅛ in (3 mm) thick, then cut into ½-in (1-cm) squares. Add half the squares, salt, pepper, cumin, and cayenne to the lentils, then cook for 15 minutes or until dough becomes a soft bread. Add lemon juice and stir. Set aside and keep hot.

In a frying pan on medium, heat olive oil and sauté onions until light brown, about 8 minutes. Stir onion into lentils.

In the same frying pan on medium heat, add 1 in (2.5 cm) vegetable oil and deep-fry remaining dough squares for 2 minutes or until golden brown. Remove with a slotted spoon and set aside.

In a bowl, combine cilantro and garlic and set aside.

Serve lentils in soup bowls. Enjoy with fried bread, cilantro-garlic mixture, and pomegranate seeds to taste.

MAKES 8 TO 10 SERVINGS

Qamih Maslouq (Qilba)

The Soul of Life

For Syrians, wheat symbolizes the soul of life. Three centuries ago, wheat gave life to the poor, who used it to make their bread and bulgur. Today, in the farming villages of Syria, this dish is common healthy fare, a good way to quickly feed a hungry stomach. Habeeb's family often relished this dish for breakfast, or even dessert, on the homestead. The distinct flavor and aroma of honey and cloves as the *qilba* boils takes you on a journey back to traditional Syria.

For the celebration of Saint Barbara in Syria, *saleeqa*—a similar dish of boiled wheat is prepared, embellished with aniseed, cinnamon, a little sugar, walnuts, and other rich nuts.

1 cup (120 g) whole wheat
  kernels, rinsed
6 cups (1.5 L) water
1 tbsp honey
6 tbsp walnut pieces
4 tbsp pine nuts

4 tbsp golden raisins, soaked
  in water for 2 hours then
  drained
2 tsp orange blossom water
¼ tsp ground cloves (optional)

In a saucepan, bring wheat and water to a boil. Reduce heat to medium, cover, and cook for 40 minutes. Stir in remaining ingredients, bring to a boil, reduce heat to medium, and cook uncovered for 3 minutes. Serve immediately.

MAKES 4 SERVINGS

Yahoudi Musaafir

The Traveler's Dish

Whenever Leila makes *yahoudi musaafir,* her family is perplexed. Why? Because her husband and children cannot understand why anyone would run away from this dish!

In Damascus in the 18th and 19th centuries, Muslims, Christian, and Jews all ate the same food, save for religious dietary restrictions. According to old tales, this dish was prepared to send off a Jewish person leaving on a trip—but it was called *Muslim harbaan,* the runaway Muslim. When the Muslims of the city heard this, they renamed the dish *yahoudi musaafir*—the traveling Jew. But all in good fun. After all, everyone still eats it today, because eggplant, tomatoes, and bulgur are nonsectarian. We recommend serving this with a bowl of *khiyaar bil-laban* (see p. 140).

6 tbsp olive oil, divided

⅓ cup (45 g) pine nuts

5 garlic cloves, minced

1 cup (50 g) finely chopped cilantro

1½ cups (340 g) coarse (#3 or #4) bulgur, rinsed and drained

1 large onion, finely chopped

1 medium red bell pepper, seeded and finely chopped

2 large ripe tomatoes, peeled and very finely chopped

½ tsp salt

¼ tsp black pepper

pinch of Aleppo pepper

1¾ cups (415 mL) boiling water

1 tbsp butter

1½ lb (750 g) eggplant, peeled, cubed, and deep-fried

In a saucepan on medium, heat 1 tbsp oil and sauté pine nuts until golden. Remove and set aside.

In the same saucepan on medium, heat 1 tbsp oil and sauté garlic for

Continues...

1 minute. Add cilantro and stir-fry for 2 minutes. Remove and set aside.

In the same saucepan on medium, heat 2 tbsp oil and stir-fry bulgur for 2 minutes, using a fork to break up any lumps. Remove and set aside.

In the same saucepan on medium, heat 2 tbsp oil and sauté onions until translucent and soft, about 10 minutes. Add in red pepper and cook, stirring constantly, for 3 to 4 minutes. Add tomatoes and their juice, garlic-cilantro mixture, salt, black pepper, and Aleppo pepper. Bring to a boil for 2 minutes, then add water and butter and bring to a boil again. Add bulgur. Reduce heat to medium, cover, and cook for 10 minutes, or until liquid is absorbed and bulgur is tender. Remove from heat. Carefully place eggplant on top, cover, and let sit for 15 minutes.

Transfer to a serving platter and decorate with toasted pine nuts.

MAKES 6 TO 8 SERVINGS

Abou Shalhoub

Zucchini with Bulgur

This dish may have been named after its creator, or according to our Palestinian friends, it's connected with the Palestinian village of Abou Shalhoub. Either way, it represents the authentic flavors of *bilaad al-shaam*. Serve this with *khiyaar bil-laban* (see p. 140).

4 tbsp olive oil

4 tbsp butter

2 lb (900 g) zucchini (or small squash), diced into ¾-in (2-cm) pieces

2 cups (500 mL) water

1 tsp salt

1 tsp black pepper

1 cup (225 g) coarse (#3 or #4) bulgur

6 garlic cloves, crushed

2 cups (100 g) chopped cilantro

In a saucepan on medium, heat oil and butter. Stir in zucchini, cover, and cook for 10 minutes, stirring occasionally. Stir in water, salt, and pepper and bring to a boil. Stir in bulgur. Bring to a boil, reduce heat to medium-low, cover, and cook for 20 minutes, stirring occasionally. Stir in garlic and cilantro and cook for 2 minutes, stirring constantly.

MAKES 6 SERVINGS

Kousa Miqleeya ma'a Dibs Rummaan

Pomegranate Squish and Squash

Pomegranates grow profusely in Syria, especially in the oasis of Palmyra. This recipe uses both the seeds and *dibs rummaan* for a unique tangy flavor.

¼ cup (60 mL) olive oil

2 large squash (or zucchini), cut into ½-in (1-cm) slices

2 tbsp *dibs rummaan*, diluted in 2 tbsp water

2 tbsp very finely chopped cilantro

2 garlic cloves, crushed

½ tsp black pepper

⅛ tsp Aleppo pepper

4 tbsp pomegranate seeds

In a frying pan on medium, heat oil and sauté squash slices for 4 to 5 minutes or until they begin to brown, turning once and adding more oil if necessary. Remove squash with a slotted spoon and place on a serving platter. For the sauce, combine remaining ingredients except pomegranate seeds, then spoon over squash slices. Let stand for 1 hour then decorate with pomegranate seeds.

MAKES 4 TO 6 SERVINGS

'Ijjat Kousa Miqleeya

Zucchini Fritters

In the 18th and 19th centuries, eggs and *kousa* were common foods for the Syrian peasantry. Eggs that weren't taken to the market to sell were used in dishes like this one.

2 cups (300 g) zucchini pulp, or peeled zucchini finely chopped

½ cup (50 g) finely chopped green onions

2 tbsp finely chopped cilantro

1 medium red bell pepper, seeded and finely chopped

5 eggs, beaten

½ cup (75 g) flour

2½ tsp baking powder

1 garlic clove, minced

1 tsp salt

½ tsp black pepper

¼ tsp *baharaat*

vegetable oil for deep-frying

Squeeze water out of pulp or chopped zucchini, then place in a mixing bowl. Add remaining ingredients except oil and mix thoroughly to make a soft batter. In a small saucepan on medium, heat 1½ in (4 cm) of oil. To test the oil, drop in tiny amount of batter; if there is no bubbling, the oil isn't ready, and if there is too much, the oil is too hot. Drop in batter by the tablespoon and fry for 3 minutes until golden, turning once. Remove fritters with a slotted spoon and drain on paper towel. Continue with the rest of the batter. Serve immediately.

MAKES 30 FRITTERS

'Ijja

Syrian Omelet

This omelet is a great way to use up zucchini pulp reserved from making *kousa mihshee* (see p. 183). *'Ijja* should be flat and thin. We use a small frying pan; a larger pan will make two big *'ijja*.

½ cup (15 g) finely chopped parsley

⅓ cup (50 g) finely chopped sweet onion

½ cup (75 g) finely chopped zucchini pulp

2 tbsp finely chopped green onions

¼ tsp salt

¼ tsp black pepper

¼ tsp sumac

¼ tsp cumin

¾ tbsp flour

7 eggs

vegetable oil for frying

In a bowl, combine all ingredients except eggs and oil. Break eggs over the contents of the bowl and mix well with a fork. In a small frying pan on medium, heat 1 tbsp oil and add a ladleful of egg mixture into the pan. Move pan in a circular motion to evenly spread the mixture. Cook on one side for 1 or 2 minutes then carefully flip and cook other side for 1 minute. Remove from pan and continue making omelets with the rest of the mixture, adding more oil to the pan as needed.

MAKES 4 TO 6 SERVINGS

Fattat Hummus

Chickpea and Yogurt Fatteh

Fatta dishes have bread as the main ingredient and are topped by yogurt sauce, but the treasure is underneath, where chicken, chickpeas, lamb, or eggplant hide. The medley of crispy and smooth layers with the crunch of fresh pomegranate seeds and hot toasted pine nuts is a sensation hard to forget. Our first taste of fatteh was at the Abu Kamal in the middle Damascus. The restaurant was jam-packed, but when we suggested we come back another day, the waiter smiled and advised us it was like that every day. Why? Because everyone loves fatteh!

2 medium loaves Arab bread, toasted and broken into small pieces

1 19-oz (540-mL) can chickpeas, drained

1 cup (250 mL) yogurt

1 garlic clove, crushed

¾ tsp salt

½ tsp black pepper

seeds of 1 pomegranate

2 tbsp lemon juice

1 tbsp tahini

2 tbsp butter

4 tbsp pine nuts or slivered almonds

2 tbsp finely chopped parsley

Spread bread pieces evenly on a platter, then spread chickpeas evenly over top and set aside. In a bowl, combine yogurt, garlic, salt, pepper, pomegranate seeds, lemon juice, and tahini, then spread over chickpeas. In a frying pan on medium-low heat, melt butter and sauté pine nuts or almonds until golden. Spoon nuts with their butter over yogurt mixture, and decorate with parsley.

MAKES 6 SERVINGS

Tasqeeya

The Lady of Ramadan

Tasqeeya is a true Damascene dish available on every street corner for iftar each day during the month of Ramadan. However, it is also made at home the rest of the year for breakfast or a late dinner. *Tasqeeya* is always accompanied by fresh radishes, quartered sweet onions, and watercress.

vegetable oil for frying

1 large loaf Arab bread

1 cup (200 g) dried chickpeas, soaked overnight in water mixed with ½ tsp baking soda, drained, and rinsed

2 large garlic cloves, crushed

4 tbsp olive oil

2 tbsp tahini

3 tbsp lemon juice

½ tsp cumin

½ tsp salt

½ tsp black pepper

¼ tsp paprika

2 tbsp finely chopped parsley

2 tbsp pine nuts, toasted in 2 tbsp butter

Split open Arab bread then cut into 1-in (2.5-cm) pieces and lightly fry in oil until golden.

In a saucepan, cover chickpeas with 2 in (2.5 cm) water. Bring to a boil, reduce heat to medium, cover, and cook for 1 hour or until chickpeas are tender. Drain chickpeas, reserving water.

Arrange bread in a serving plate with deep edges. Spread 1½ cups (245 g) chickpeas evenly over top. Pour 1 cup (250 mL) reserved chickpea water over top. Set aside.

In a food processor, blend remaining chickpeas, ½ cup (125 mL) chickpea

Continues...

water, garlic, oil, tahini, lemon juice, cumin, salt, and pepper until creamy smooth.

Pour chickpea mixture over serving plate, sprinkle with paprika and parsley, spoon pine nuts with their butter over top, and serve immediately.

MAKES 6 SERVINGS

Kubba Heela Haamid

Impostor Kibbeh

Syrian folklore credits this dish to a poor woman who wanted to make kibbeh for her family who had been craving it for some time. Desperate, she looked in her near-barren cupboard and only found bulgur, onions, and olive oil. She did her best and presented the dish to her family, not mentioning once that this was the "impostor" version. During the 18th and 19th centuries, when peasants depended on bulgur and other inexpensive staples, this dish was a full and hearty meal. Even today, the city of Homs proudly proclaims that it makes the best *kubba heela haamid*.

Stuffing

4 tablespoons olive oil

1 large onion, finely chopped

4 tablespoons pine nuts

½ teaspoon salt

½ teaspoon black pepper

Kubba dough

1 cup (225 g) fine (#1) bulgur, soaked
    in water for 1 hour, then drained
    by pressing out all its water

½ cup (75 g) flour

1 medium onion, chopped

½ teaspoon salt

½ teaspoon black pepper

½ teaspoon paprika

½ teaspoon *baharaat*

⅛ teaspoon Aleppo pepper

Sauce

8 cups (2 L) water

½ teaspoon salt

Continues...

½ teaspoon black pepper

½ teaspoon paprika

½ teaspoon *baharaat*

2 tablespoons *dibs rummaan*

2 tablespoons lemon juice

6 cloves garlic, crushed

For the stuffing: In a frying pan on medium, heat oil and sauté remaining ingredients for 8 minutes. Set aside.

For the *kubba* dough: In a deep bowl, mix all ingredients by hand. Transfer mixture to a food processor and blend until mixture forms slightly sticky dough. Divide into 2 portions.

Dip hands slightly in cold water, take 1 portion of dough, form marble-sized balls, and place on a tray. Cover with a kitchen towel and set aside.

For the remaining portion of dough, form ball about the size of a golf ball and place it in the palm of your hand. Use the forefinger of the other hand to make an indentation. Expand the hollow by rotating and pressing the ball against the palm of your hand until it is ¼ in (6 mm) deep. Place one heaping tablespoon of stuffing in the hollow, then close it up and form into an egg shape. Dip your fingers in a bowl of cold water with a sprinkling of salt to help smooth it out. Repeat until all dough is used. Place the stuffed *kubba* on a tray and cover with a tea towel.

Let the *kubba* balls and stuffed *kubba* sit for 1 hour.

For the sauce: In a large saucepan, bring all ingredients to a boil, then carefully add *kubba* balls and stuffed *kubba,* stirring gently.

Reduce heat to medium, cover, and cook for 40 minutes, gently stirring occasionally. Serve hot.

MAKES 6 TO 8 SERVINGS

Kubbat Bataata

Potato Kibbeh

One of the most popular types of vegetarian kibbeh is made with potatoes, with the spices varying from country to country. Although we present a vegetarian stuffing here, a meat filling, such as *kubba* stuffing, can be substituted (see p. 168). Serve this hot or cold with yogurt and *salatat hindba* (see p. 139).

1½ cups (375 g) fine (#1) bulgur

4 cups (1.3 kg) mashed potatoes (with no added ingredients)

4 tbsp flour

1 tsp dried basil

½ tsp allspice

½ tsp cinnamon

½ tsp cumin

¼ tsp cayenne

3 cups (450 g) finely chopped onions, divided

2 tsp salt, divided

1 tsp black pepper, divided

6 tbsp olive oil, divided

4 garlic cloves, minced

2 tbsp finely chopped cilantro

¾ cup (100 g) pine nuts or slivered almonds

Soak bulgur in warm water for 15 minutes, then press out water through a fine mesh strainer.

In a large mixing bowl, combine bulgur, potatoes, flour, basil, allspice, cinnamon, cumin, cayenne, 1 cup (150 g) onions, 1½ tsp salt, and ½ tsp pepper, then divide into 2 even portions and set aside.

In a frying pan on medium, heat 4 tbsp oil and sauté remaining onions with garlic, cilantro, and nuts for 10 minutes. Stir in remaining salt and pepper and set aside.

Continues...

Preheat oven to 400°F (200°C).

Spread one portion of potato mixture evenly in a greased 9 x 13-in (3.5-L) casserole dish, then spread frying pan contents evenly on top. Spread other portion of potato mixture on top and smooth it out. Cut into 2 x 2-in (5 x 5-cm) squares, then drizzle with remaining oil.

Bake for 40 minutes or until edges turn golden brown. If top is not brown, place under the broiler for 5 minutes or until light brown.

MAKES 10 TO 12 SERVINGS

Kubbat Laqteen

Pumpkin Kibbeh

The day after trick or treating, while their friends were enjoying their Halloween candy, Leila and Muna would be munching on their mother's *kubbat laqteen* without fail.

1 cup (225 g) fine (#1) bulgur

6 tbsp olive oil, divided

2 large onions, finely chopped, divided

4 garlic cloves, minced

½ cup (70 g) pine nuts, toasted

2 cups (330 g) cooked (or canned) chickpeas

1½ tsp salt, divided

¾ tsp black pepper, divided

¾ tsp coriander, divided

¾ tsp allspice, divided

¾ tsp cumin, divided

¾ tsp paprika, divided

2 cups (450 g) mashed baked pumpkin

1 cup (90 g) very fine bread crumbs

⅛ tsp cayenne

Soak bulgur in hot water for 10 minutes, then press out water through a fine mesh strainer.

In a frying pan on medium, heat 4 tbsp oil and sauté half the onions for 8 minutes. Add garlic, pine nuts, chickpeas, and a ¼ tsp each of salt, pepper, coriander, allspice, cumin, and paprika, then sauté for 3 minutes. Remove from heat and allow to cool.

Preheat oven to 400°F (200°C).

In a bowl, thoroughly mix all remaining ingredients except remaining oil. Divide pumpkin mixture into two equal portions. Flatten one portion in a

Continues...

greased 9-in (2.5-L) square baking pan. Spread frying pan contents evenly on top, then cover with remaining pumpkin mixture. Cut into 8 pieces then drizzle remaining oil over top. Bake for 50 minutes or until golden. Serve warm or cold.

MAKES 8 SERVINGS

Loubya bil-Zayt

Green Beans in Oil

Nothing could be tastier than a dish of fresh green beans, tomatoes, and onions cooked in olive oil. It is also a perfect side dish with any entrée. Scoop up the beans with a hefty piece of fresh Arab bread topped with slivers of raw onion and a squeeze of lemon.

4 tbsp olive oil

2 medium onions, thinly sliced

8 garlic cloves, minced

1 lb (500 g) green beans, snapped and halved

4 large tomatoes, peeled and chopped in small pieces

1 tsp salt

½ tsp black pepper

In a saucepan on medium, heat oil and sauté onion and garlic until onions are limp and translucent, about 10 to 12 minutes. Add beans and stir-fry for 5 minutes. Stir in tomatoes. Season with salt and pepper. Cover and cook for 30 minutes, stirring often. Uncover and cook for 15 to 20 minutes, stirring occasionally. Adjust seasoning.

Transfer to a serving platter and serve hot or cold.

MAKES 6 TO 8 SERVINGS

Bouraanee

Spinach with Yogurt

In the mid-18th century, Alexander Russell, chief medical practitioner to the British Levant Company, noted that the Arabs did not believe there was any place on earth where yogurt was not found. There was always yogurt on every Syrian table, served either on its own or mixed with greens or herbs. Serve this with toasted Arab bread.

2 lb (900 g) baby spinach, washed thoroughly	¼ tsp cinnamon
1½ cups (375 mL) yogurt	¼ tsp allspice
4 garlic cloves, crushed	¼ tsp black pepper
1 tsp salt	½ cup (25 g) finely chopped cilantro
6 tbsp olive oil	¼ cup (30 g) chopped walnuts
½ tsp baharaat	¼ cup (35 g) pine nuts, toasted

In a large saucepan on medium heat, add spinach, cover, and cook for 5 minutes, or until wilted. Remove spinach, drain any water, and set aside.

In a bowl, combine yogurt, garlic, and salt. Set aside.

In a large frying pan on medium-high, heat oil and sauté spinach, spices, and cilantro for 5 minutes, stirring constantly.

Transfer spinach mixture to a serving platter. Spoon yogurt mixture over top. Sprinkle with walnuts and pine nuts.

MAKES 6 SERVINGS

Although *bouraanee* has been popular since the medieval period, Damascus's version is unique in that it uses spinach instead of the original eggplant. Aleppo enjoys the same dish under the name *al-sabaanikheeya*. *Bouraanee* can also be made as a meat dish to which cilantro and garlic are added at the end. Yes, we could have included the *bouraanee* with meat, but we felt our vegetarian friends deserved to enjoy this generations-old delicious dish of Damascus.

Yaalanjee

Vegetarian Stuffed Grape Leaves

Yaalanjee look like *yabraq* (see
p. 185) but are made with oil
instead of butter so that they
can be eaten hot or cold. The
word *yaalanjee* is from the
Turkish *yalanci dolma*, *yalanci*
meaning "imitation" to describe
the meatless stuffing. Its meat,
some say, is the onions in it.

One Syrian folktale insists the name of this dish came about as a mis-understanding. There was a woman who was unable to speak, so she and her husband communicated in writing or with hand gestures. One day, while she was busy rolling grape leaves, her husband walked in and pointed to the pot to ask her what she was making. Thinking he wanted to know when lunch would be ready, she wrote in the easiest form of col-loquial Arabic, *Yalla njee*— "We're on our way!" But in her haste, the two words looked like one. We're pretty sure when the aroma of the herbs and spices wafts from the pot of *yaalanjee*, everyone will be on their way!

1 16-oz (454-g) jar preserved
  grape leaves, or equivalent
  amount of fresh leaves

1 cup (200 g) basmati or other
  long-grain white rice, soaked
  for 1 hour then drained

2 cups (50 g) finely chopped
  parsley

1 cup (100 g) finely chopped
  green onions

1 medium tomato, peeled and
  finely chopped

1 medium onion, finely chopped

1 tsp allspice

1 tsp dried mint, crushed

1 tsp black pepper

1½ tsp salt

pinch of cayenne

½ cup (125 mL) + 1 tbsp olive oil

½ cup (125 mL) + 1 tbsp lemon
  juice

If using preserved grape leaves, drain leaves then place in a bowl and cover with boiling water. Let sit for 15 minutes, then rinse and drain in colander.

Continues...

If using fresh leaves, place in a bowl and cover with boiling water and let sit for 1 minute. Trim stems and shake off any excess water.

Meanwhile, prepare the stuffing: in a bowl, mix remaining ingredients, ½ cup (125 mL) olive oil, and ½ cup (125 mL) lemon juice.

Place a few grape leaves on a flat work surface, shiny side down with the stem end facing you. Snip off the tough stems.

Place 1 tsp stuffing (depending on size of leaf) lengthwise at bottom of leaf but not touching the edges. Roll grape leaf over stuffing, folding in the edges after the first roll, and then continue to roll the leaf tightly. Continue until all leaves are rolled.

In a large saucepan, place rolled grape leaves seam side down in compact rows, alternating the direction of the rolls every other row. Use smaller rolls to fill in any gaps in the layers. Pour any remaining liquid from the stuffing over the rolls.

Place an inverted plate over rolls, pressing down slightly, to keep the rolls intact. Cover with water reaching almost to the top of the plate. Cover and cook on medium heat for 30 minutes or until leaves are tender and rice is cooked. Remove plate and reduce heat to medium-low. Drizzle remaining oil and lemon juice over rolls, cover, and cook for 15 minutes. Remove from heat and let stand for 10 minutes.

Drain any excess liquid. Unmold rolls by placing a serving dish over the saucepan and inverting, placing any fallen rolls back in place. Garnish with lemon slices.

MAKES 6 TO 8 SERVINGS

Savory Pies

Fataayir bil-Kishk

Kishk Pies

Throughout Syria and the Middle East, *fataayir* are pastry pies that encase various meat, vegetable, or cheese fillings. Closed or open, triangular, square, or half-moon shaped, they're hearty finger food for those in need of a quick savory bite. Nothing gets the stomach going more than the aroma of freshly baked *fataayir* filling the morning air of Old Damascus. Hot, spicy, and satisfying, these savory pies awaken the soul.

Simply omit the *qawarma* or meat to make these pies vegetarian.

1 recipe *'ajeenat al-fataayir* (see p. 50)

1 cup (100 g) *kishk* (see p. 59)

1 cup (250 mL) water

¾ cup (115 g) *qawarma*, fat removed (see p. 62), or very small pieces of fried meat

1 small bunch green onions, finely chopped

1 tsp salt

½ tsp black pepper

½ cup (125 mL) olive oil

¼ cup (60 mL) vegetable oil or melted butter for brushing

Form *'ajeenat al-fataayir* (dough) into 12 balls. Cover with plastic wrap or a tea towel and let rest for 30 minutes.

Meanwhile, make the filling. In a bowl, mix *kishk* with water, then add remaining ingredients except oil or butter for brushing and combine thoroughly. Divide filling into 12 portions and set aside.

Preheat oven to 400°F (200°C).

Roll out each ball into a circle 5 to 6 in (12 to 15 cm) wide, then place a portion of filling in the middle. Fold edges of circle over filling toward the center to make a triangle, then close firmly by pinching edges together. Continue until all balls are finished.

Place pies on greased baking trays, lightly brush tops with oil or butter, and bake for 10 to 15 minutes or until pies are golden. If desired, brown further under the broiler for 1 to 2 minutes. Brush tops of the pies lightly with more oil or butter and serve hot.

MAKES 12 PIES

Fataayir bil-Labna ma'a Qawarma

Labna and *Qawarma* Pies

Habeeb remembers his mother often sending him to bring piping-hot *fataayir bil-labna ma'a qawarma* to his father in the fields. Seeing Habeeb approach, his father would drop his tools, so happy to receive this fragrant package. After the first bite he would say, "Even in Syria, no one makes them as good your mom."

1 recipe *'ajeenat al-fataayir* (see p. 50)

1 cup (150 g) *qawarma*, fat removed (see p. 62)

labna (see p. 58) (cream cheese can be substituted)

1 medium onion, finely chopped

1 tsp salt

1 tsp black pepper

1 tbsp sumac (optional)

¼ cup (60 mL) vegetable oil for brushing

Form *'ajeenat al-fataayir* (dough) into 12 balls. Cover with plastic wrap or a tea towel and let rest for 30 minutes.

Meanwhile, make the filling: in a bowl, thoroughly combine remaining ingredients except oil and set aside.

Preheat oven to 400°F (200°C).

Roll out balls into circles 5 to 6 in (12 to 15 cm) wide, or larger if desired. Place one heaping tablespoon of filling on each circle, then fold edges over filling to make a triangle and close firmly by pinching edges.

Place pies on greased baking trays and brush tops lightly with oil. Bake for 20 minutes or until pies are golden. If desired, brown further under the broiler for 1 to 2 minutes. Brush tops of pies lightly with more oil and serve hot straight from the oven or at room temperature.

MAKES 12 PIES

Fataayir bil-Sabaanikh

Spinach Pies

Syrian cuisine has included stuffed pies since part of the region was known as Mesopotamia. In fact, a recipe for a two-crust pie stuffed with onions, leeks, garlic, and the meat of little birds appears on an ancient Babylonian tablet. Fast-forward to 1905, when spinach "fotiyer" was characteristic of the Syrian Colony in New York. Habeeb's version differs slightly from tradition with the addition of feta cheese to the filling for a creamy texture.

1 recipe *'ajeenat al-fataayir* (see p. 50)

1 lb (454 g) spinach, washed and finely chopped

2 medium onions, finely chopped

½ cup (75 g) crumbled feta cheese (optional)

1 tbsp pine nuts

4 tbsp olive oil

2 tbsp lemon juice

2 tbsp sumac

¾ tsp salt

½ tsp black pepper

½ tsp nutmeg

⅛ tsp cayenne

¼ cup (60 mL) vegetable oil for brushing

Form *'ajeenat al-fataayir* (dough) into 12 balls. Place on a floured surface, cover with plastic wrap or a tea towel, and let rest for 30 minutes.

Meanwhile, make the filling: in a bowl, thoroughly combine remaining

Continues...

ingredients except oil for brushing and set aside in a colander. Let sit for 15 minutes to drain excess liquid.

Preheat oven to 400°F (200°C).

Roll out balls into circles 6 in (15 cm) wide. Working with one circle at a time, place two heaping tablespoons of filling in the middle, making sure filling doesn't touch the edges. Fold dough over the filling into a half-moon or triangle shape and close by firmly pinching edges together. Put a little flour on your fingertips when you press the edges closed to help them stick.

Place pies on well-greased baking trays and bake for 20 minutes or until pies are golden. Brush tops of pies with oil and serve hot or cold.

MAKES 12 PIES

Manaqeesh bil-Za'tar

Thyme and Sumac Round Flatbread

This savory flatbread is the most popular breakfast item in Greater Syria. Women used to rise early to make dough to have *manaqeesh* ready for the morning meal, but now the trend is to go to the neighborhood bakery and pick them up fresh and hot. Accompaniments of sliced tomatoes, cucumbers, green onions, *labna* (see p. 58), and fresh mint make this flatbread the perfect and complete Syrian breakfast.

1 recipe *'ajeenat al-fataayir* (see p. 50)	1 tsp dried marjoram
3 tbsp dried thyme	½ tsp salt
4 tbsp sumac	¼ tsp cayenne
2 tbsp sesame seeds, toasted	½ cup (125 mL) olive oil for brushing

Form *'ajeenat al-fataayir* (dough) into 12 balls. Place on a tray dusted with flour, cover with plastic wrap or a tea towel, and let rest in a warm place for 15 minutes.

Meanwhile, make the topping: in a bowl, thoroughly mix remaining ingredients except oil for brushing, and set aside.

Preheat oven to 400°F (200°C).

Roll out balls into circles ⅛ in (3 mm) thick, then place on greased baking trays. Divide topping into 12 equal portions. Take one portion and with

Continues...

the back of a spoon spread it over a circle, leaving an edge of ¼ in (6 mm). To secure the topping on the dough, press topping gently with fingertips to make little indentations, making sure that topping does not reach the edge. Bake for 20 minutes or until edges are light brown. Brush the edges lightly with oil.

Serve hot (or cold, but hot is better). If not going to be eaten immediately, brush *manaqeesh* lightly with more oil and reheat just before serving.

MAKES 12 FLATBREADS

For a different take on manaqeesh bil-za'tar, try a few with the following topping (ingredients are for 4 flatbreads only):

1/2 cup (35 g) za'atar
1/2 cup (115 g) finely chopped tomatoes
1/2 cup (75 g) finely chopped onion
1/2 cup (125 mL) olive oil
juice of 1/2 lemon

Some enjoy a little more lemon juice squeezed over their fresh-baked pie before eating it.

Sfeeha bil-Lahm

Open-Faced Meat Pies

Syrians who migrated early to South America brought their *sfeeha* with them. Today, in Brazil they are a common street food known as *esfíha* or *esfirra*.

In the mid-18th century, by the end of August, Aleppo's gardens and orchards were replete with pomegranates. Households would stockpile them for winter use, by drying the seeds or preparing the juice as a replacement for vinegar or verjuice. So plentiful was this fruit that Aleppan dishes were almost incomplete without it. An 18th-century visitor to Syria described *sfeeha* as "mincemeat with pomegranate grains, spread upon thin cakes, and baked on an iron plate"—and it remains one of the most popular savory pies in Greater Syria today, with Aleppo still taking top prize. Serve this with a side dish of yogurt.

one recipe *'ajeenat al-fataayir* (see p. 50)

1 lb (500 g) ground lamb or beef with some fat

2 cups (350 g) pomegranate seeds

2 medium onions, very finely chopped

4 garlic cloves, crushed

½ cup (15 g) finely chopped parsley

2 medium tomatoes, finely chopped

2 tbsp tomato paste

1 tbsp *dibs rummaan*

2 tbsp yogurt

1 tsp *baharaat*

1 tsp salt

½ tsp black pepper

½ tsp coriander

⅛ tsp Aleppo pepper

4 tbsp olive oil for brushing

1 lemon

Continues...

Form *'ajeenat al-fataayir* (dough) into 18 balls. Cover with a plastic wrap or a tea towel and let rest for 1 hour.

Meanwhile, make the topping: in a bowl, thoroughly combine remaining ingredients except the lemon and oil for brushing. Divide topping into 18 portions and set aside.

Preheat oven to 400°F (200°C).

Roll dough balls into circles about 5 in (12 cm) wide and place on greased baking trays. Place topping in the middle of the circles and gently press down evenly with fingertips. Flute the edges to hold in any meat juices.

Bake for 20 minutes, or until edges begin to brown. Remove pies from the oven and brush edges with a little oil. Sprinkle lemon juice over top for some tartness.

MAKES 18 PIES

Desserts

· · · · · · · · · · · · ·

Baraazik

Crispy Sesame Cookies

A speciality of Damascus, these small, round, crispy sesame cookies have been peddled on the city streets for centuries.

¾ cup (112 g) sesame seeds

½ cup (125 mL) honey

½ cup (50 g) coarsely chopped pistachios

2 eggs

1½ cups (340 g) unsalted butter

1½ cups (300 g) sugar

2½ cups (375 g) flour

2 cups (330 g) wheat hearts or fine semolina

2 tsp baking powder

½ tsp salt

Place sesame seeds, honey, and pistachios in separate bowls and set aside.

In a food processor, mix eggs, butter, and sugar. Transfer to a mixing bowl and add flour, wheat hearts or semolina, baking powder, and salt. Knead into a smooth, but not sticky dough, adding a little water if necessary.

Preheat oven to 350°F (180°C).

Form dough into 40 walnut-sized balls, then dip balls—on one side only, one at a time, into the pistachios and flatten with fingers. Place cookies, pistachio side down, on greased baking trays. Brush each cookie lightly with honey and sprinkle with sesame seeds.

Bake for 15 minutes or until cookies are golden brown, then remove and let cool before serving.

MAKES 40 COOKIES

Baqlaawa

Baklava

Damascus is the city of sweets, renowned throughout history for its confections, candied fruits, and fritters. In 1799, when French troops ransacked the tents of Arab soldiers during Napoleon's Syrian campaign, they "found there such quantities of Damascus sweets and cakes, renowned throughout the Orient, that they filled their pockets, their haver sacks ... instead of getting some rest they passed the night in celebration, dancing and singing and delivering the most heartfelt eulogies to the confectioners of Damascus as they gorged on their sweets." A century later, the *New York Times* described baklava as Syria's "national dish of pastry," standing "in place of the great American pie." Layers of crisp, buttery phyllo with a rich nut filling and covered with sweet sugar syrup—no other dessert is so tempting.

Habeeb's mother, Shams, and his late wife, Fareeda, both made their own phyllo dough from scratch, as did their mothers and grandmothers in the Qaraoun and Damascus. Holidays have always been synonymous with baklava. When the wedding rings came off to avoid tearing the paper-thin sheets of hand-stretched phyllo, and only those making it were allowed in the kitchen. This was an all-day process in which a ball of dough would eventually turn out four trays of golden, sweet, nut-filled pastry. Purportedly, in the 8th century, Umayyad Caliph Sulayman ibn Abd al-Malik could eat 20 lb (9 kg) of *kunaafa*, a very thin pastry just like phyllo, in one sitting. We don't blame him!

2 cups (250 g) walnuts, chopped

1 cup (200 g) sugar

2 cups (500 mL) melted unsalted butter, divided

1 tbsp orange blossom water

1 lb (500 g) phyllo dough, thawed

1 recipe *qatr* (see p. 69)

For the filling: in a mixing bowl, combine walnuts, sugar, ¼ cup (57 g) butter, and orange blossom water, then set aside.

Butter a 10 x 15-in (4-L), or 9 x 13-in (3.5-L) baking dish for a thicker baklava, and set aside.

Remove phyllo sheets from package, unroll, and spread on a kitchen towel. Cover sheets with plastic wrap to prevent drying out. Working quickly with the

Continues...

phyllo, take one sheet and place in the baking dish (if using a 9 x 13-in [3.5-L] baking dish, fold in any overlap toward the dish), then brush with butter. Repeat until ½ package is used.

Spread filling evenly over buttered phyllo.

Take one sheet of the remaining phyllo, place it over the filling, and gently brush it with butter. Repeat with remaining sheets. Spoon remaining butter evenly over top.

Preheat oven to 400°F (200°C).

With a sharp knife, carefully cut baklava into 2-in (5-cm) squares or diamonds. Bake for 5 minutes, then reduce temperature to 300°F (180°C) and bake for 45 minutes, or until the pastry is crisp and the edges are golden. For a golden top, broil for 1 to 2 minutes.

Pour *qatr* evenly over hot baklava. Let sit for 2 hours, then serve.

MAKES 24 TO 36 PIECES

Ghurayba

Syrian Shortbread

The Arabs introduced this cookie, which became the famous *polvorones* of Spain, to the Iberian Peninsula when they conquered and settled there in the 8th century. During the Spanish Inquisition, the inquisitors in southern Spain declared that *polvorones* were to be made with pork fat instead of butter. Those who made them with the latter were then convicted of being secret Muslims or secret Jews.

Ghurayba, or "little strange things," are slightly sweet, crumbly butter cookies. Its continuity through the centuries is proof of its popularity.

1½ cups (340 g) unsalted butter (at room temperature)

1¾ cups (218 g) confectioner's sugar, divided

1 tsp orange blossom water

1 egg yolk

3 cups (450 g) flour

40 blanched almonds

Preheat oven to 300°F (150°C).

With an electric mixer, blend butter, 1½ cups (187 g) confectioner's sugar, orange blossom water, and egg yolk until smooth. Transfer to a mixing bowl and gradually add flour, mixing with your fingers to form smooth dough. Dough should be soft but not stick to your hands.

Form dough into 40 balls, a little smaller than a walnut. Place on ungreased baking trays and flatten to ½ in (1 cm) thickness. Press an almond into each cookie and bake for 20 minutes or until bottoms are light brown. The *ghurayba* may feel soft at the end of the baking time, but they will harden as they cool. Remove from oven, let cool completely on trays and then dust them with remaining confectioner's sugar.

For a different shape, try pressing dough into a mold, like *ma'moul bil-tamar* (see p. 295). The number of cookies will depend on the size of the mold.

MAKES 40 COOKIES

Ma'moul bil-Tamar

Date-Stuffed Shortbread

Ma'moul Tips

Fill *ma'moul* with dates, pistachios, or walnuts. (Although in the Salloum family, we use semolina dough for nut-filled *ma'moul*.) Sprinkle icing sugar over cookies with nut stuffing, after they have cooled. Leave date-filled cookies as they are.

For extra flavor, add a few tablespoons of orange blossom water or mahaleb to the dough.

Purchase *ma'moul* molds at Middle Eastern markets. The molds are made from either wood or plastic. We prefer the wood ones because they are more traditional and seem to last forever. The shapes vary, but for date-stuffed cookies round molds are best.

The distinctive sound of wooden *ma'moul* molds banging on flat surfaces to release the cookies before they enter the oven is the sign that Eid al-Adha, Christmas, or Easter is around the corner. The aroma of mahaleb permeates the kitchen on the day of baking and even the next, which rings in the holidays! Festivities are not complete without mounds of these date-stuffed cookies for family and guests to indulge in. You will need to put aside about an hour to make them, but it's time well spent.

Filling

1 lb (500 g) pitted dates, chopped

¼ cup (60 mL) melted butter

1 tsp sugar

½ cup (125 mL) water

Dough

2 cups (400 g) sugar

4 eggs

1 lb (500 g) unsalted margarine, at room temperature

1 lb (500 g) unsalted butter, at room temperature

10 cups (1.5 kg) flour

2 tbsp *mahaleb*

For the filling: In a saucepan on low heat, cook all ingredients for 10 minutes or until dates have completely softened, adding more water if necessary and stirring occasionally. Remove from heat and let cool completely.

For the dough: In a large bowl, use an electric mixer to beat sugar, eggs, margarine, and butter until smooth. Then add flour and mahaleb by hand and knead into a soft dough.

Continues...

Preheat oven to 400°F (200°C).

Break off a walnut-sized ball of dough. With your forefinger, make a hollow and insert 1 tsp filling. Close opening, making sure to keep the ball shape, then place ball in the *ma'moul* mold. Gently press down, then flip the cookie onto a baking tray. Continue until entire dough is used.

Bake cookies on middle rack until bottoms are light brown, about 15 minutes. Broil for 2 to 3 minutes until golden on top. Remove from oven and let cool, then transfer to a serving platter.

MAKES 48 TO 60 COOKIES, DEPENDING ON SIZE OF MOLD

Karabeej Halab

Whips of Aleppo

Fruit sugar, or fructose, is granulated and looks much like table sugar but is much sweeter, so less is needed. You can buy fruit sugar at health food stores or well-stocked grocery stores. You can substitute regular sugar at a ratio of 3 to 1.

These signature cookies of Aleppo, a special type of *ma'moul* (see p. 295), are dipped into *naatif*, a very sweet, fluffy marshmallow-like confection. Many of the city's pastry specialists still make it the traditional way, using the root of the soap bark tree, gradually adding *qatr* (see p. 69), and then beating to form a light, sticky mousse. *Naatif* is not a new invention. In the 10th century, some *naatif* in Syria was made from carobs. In the 14th century, a traveler to Damascus noted that the northern door of the Umayyad Mosque was known as the "Door of the *Naatif*-Makers." The following recipe is as close in taste and texture as we could get to traditional *naatif*.

Cookies

1 tbsp sugar
¼ cup (60 mL) warm water
1¼-oz (7-g) package active dry yeast
½ cup (50 g) finely ground pistachios
¼ cup (50 g) fruit sugar
1½ tbsp water
1 tsp rose water
1 lb (500 g) fine semolina
½ cup (113 g) butter, softened
½ cup (100 g) sugar
1 tsp mahaleb
¼ cup (60 mL) warm milk

Naatif

2 egg whites
¾ cup (150 g) sugar
2 tbsp cold water
2 drops white vinegar
pinch of salt

Continues...

Dissolve sugar in water, then sprinkle in yeast and stir. Cover and let sit in a warm place for 10 minutes, until yeast begins to froth.

For the filling: in a bowl, combine pistachios, fruit sugar, water, and rose water, then set aside.

For the dough: In another bowl, with your fingertips, mix semolina, butter, sugar, and mahaleb, making sure butter is mixed in well. Form a well, then pour in milk and activated yeast. Knead into a dough, then cover with plastic and refrigerate for 30 minutes.

Preheat oven to 300°F (150°C).

Form dough into walnut-sized balls. With your forefinger, form a hollow in each ball. Place 1 tsp filling in each hollow, then pinch to close. Shape balls into cylinders, then place on greased baking trays and pat down into an oval shape.

Bake for 20 minutes or until slightly brown. Allow to cool, then place on serving platter.

For the *naatif:* In a mixing bowl, beat egg whites until fluffy. Beat in remaining ingredients and keep beating for 5 minutes or until fluffy. Cover and refrigerate until needed. *Naatif* is best used within 2 days. Makes 2 cups (500 mL).

Dip whips of Aleppo into a bowl of *naatif. Naatif* can be replaced with whipped marshmallow or whipped cream.

MAKES 30 TO 35 COOKIES

Mushabbak

Lattice Fritters

Mushabbak were originally called *zalaabeeya* (see p. 304), the generic Arabic name for deep-fried dough dipped in honey. As the form of the fritter became more intricate, they were called *zalaabeeya mushab-baka*—lattice-shaped fritters, which was eventually shortened to *mushabbak*. But we think the northeastern Syrian province of al-Hasakah has given them the perfect name: *teeb wa naahee*—the Delicious and the Ultimate!

1 tbsp sugar
1¼ cups (310 mL) warm water, divided
1¼-oz (7-g) package active dry yeast
1 cup (150 g) flour

¾ cup (95 g) cornstarch
⅛ tsp salt
1 egg white
vegetable oil for deep-frying
1 recipe *qatr* (see p. 69)

Dissolve sugar in ¼ cup (60 mL) water, then sprinkle in yeast and stir. Cover and let sit in a warm place for 10 minutes or until yeast begins to froth.

In a deep mixing bowl, combine flour, cornstarch, and salt. In another bowl, beat egg white until stiff. Form a well in flour mixture and add activated yeast, remaining water, and egg white. With an electric mixer, beat for 1 minute to make a smooth batter.

Cover bowl and let sit for 1 hour to allow batter to rise, then stir.

In a deep saucepan on medium, heat enough oil for deep-frying. Using a funnel, place a finger under the narrow opening and spoon 3 tbsp batter into

Continues...

desserts · 301

the top. Hold the funnel over the saucepan, release your finger, and dribble batter into the oil by quickly moving the funnel to create a lattice shape. Fry for 2 to 3 minutes or until golden on both sides.

Remove from oil, shaking gently to remove excess oil, and immerse in *qatr*, making sure to coat both sides.

MAKES 18 TO 20 FRITTERS

Ode to *Mushabbak*
From the 10th-century Arab cookbook *Kitab al-Tabikh*

Yellow, white and colored, fried in oil of sesame ground;

Soft to touch and delicate, drenched in white thinned honey profound;

Arranged in rows like pieces of gold, like golden canes women around

One another intertwined with the other, as embroidered silk cloth together bound

In white sugar, they are buried, they are veiled from the eyes that surround;

They are delicate and dainty to the bite and when they are downed.

Al-Mushabbak al-Souree

Semolina Spiral Fritters

These sweet semolina fritters are an extra-crunchy version of the popular *mushabbak* (see p. 301).

1½ cups (300 g) medium semolina	1 cup (250 mL) warm water
1 cup (150 g) flour	vegetable oil for deep-frying
1 tsp baking powder	1 recipe *qatr* (see p. 69)
1 cup (250 mL) yogurt	¼ cup (25 g) crushed pistachios

In a deep bowl, mix semolina, flour, and baking powder, then add yogurt and water, mixing well. Cover and let stand for 1 hour.

In a saucepan on medium, heat enough oil for deep-frying. Attach a large star tip to a piping bag and spoon in some batter. Carefully squeeze batter into the oil in the form of a spiral, starting with the middle of the spiral, swirl the batter out. The cook's discretion and artistic skill determines the size of each *mushabbak* swirl. Deep-fry for 3 minutes, turning once, so that both sides are golden brown.

Have *qatr* ready at room temperature in a wide bowl. Lift fritter with a slotted spoon to drain excess oil, then immediately place in syrup for 1 minute. Remove fritter and let excess syrup drip back into bowl. Transfer to a serving platter and sprinkle with pistachios.

MAKES 8 TO 10 FRITTERS

Zalaabeeya

Fareeda's Fritters

This is Fareeda Salloum's *zalaabeeya* recipe, one she learned from her mother, Nabeeha, which was passed down through the generations of her family in Damascus. Funnily enough, Habeeb's mother, Shams, who was born in the village of Qaraoun, about 100 miles west of Damascus, had the exact same recipe for this light fritter.

Although sugar and honey are the traditional sweeteners for this fritter, as Canadian Syrians we have discovered that maple syrup pairs beautifully with *zalaabeeya*.

1 tbsp sugar
¼ cup (60 mL) warm water
1 ¼-oz (7-g) package active dry yeast
2 cups (300 g) flour
½ tsp salt

2 tbsp oil
½ cup (125 mL) water
vegetable oil for deep-frying
sugar for sprinkling
honey for dipping (optional)

Dissolve sugar in ¼ cup (60 mL) warm water, then add in yeast and stir. Cover and let sit in a warm place for 10 minutes or until yeast begins to froth.

In a mixing bowl, mix flour and salt. Form a well in the middle, then add activated yeast, oil, and ½ cup (125 mL) water. Knead into a soft, sticky dough, adding a little water or flour if necessary. Cover and let sit for 1 hour or until dough doubles in size.

Gently punch down dough. Divide into 12 balls and with the palm of your hand, roll and stretch each ball into flattened cigar-shaped pieces about 6 in (15 cm) long and 1½ in (4 cm) wide. If necessary, dip fingers lightly in flour to make handling dough easier. Cover with a tea towel and let sit for 15 minutes.

In a saucepan on medium-high, heat enough oil for deep-frying. Deep-fry dough pieces for 3 minutes or until golden all over. Drain on paper towel, then while still warm, sprinkle lightly with sugar. Serve immediately with honey for dipping.

MAKES 12 FRITTERS

'Awaymaat

The Judge's Morsels

'Awaymaat means floaters, because these tasty tidbits float to the top of the oil when cooked. But in a 13th-century Arabic cookbook, they were known as *luqmaat al-qaadee* (the judge's morsels). You can buy these fritters from open-air stalls in the heart of Old Damascus, sizzling hot from the oil and dripping with syrup.

2 cups (300 g) flour
4 tbsp cornstarch
½ tsp salt
1¼-oz (7-g) package active dry
    yeast, dissolved in ¼ cup
    (60 mL) lukewarm water

2 cups (500 mL) warm water
vegetable oil for deep-frying
1 recipe *qatr* (see p. 69)

In a mixing bowl, combine flour, cornstarch, and salt, then pour in activated yeast and mix well. Add water and stir until mixture resembles pancake batter, adding more water if necessary. Cover and set aside for 1 hour.

In a saucepan on medium, heat enough oil for deep-frying. Wet a tablespoon with cold water, scoop up batter by the tablespoon, and drop into hot oil. Cook until dough balls swell, float to the top, and are golden and crisp on all sides.

Remove with a slotted spoon and drain on paper towel for 1 minute. Dip into room-temperature *qatr* (sugar syrup), then remove with slotted spoon and arrange on a serving platter. These treats are best eaten the same day.

MAKES 36 MORSELS

Isnaan al-'Ajouz

The Old Man's Teeth

The name of this dish is misleading, considering its crunchy, light, and delicious sweetness. Samira, one of our close friends from Damascus, offered us this recipe. She remembers her grandmother telling the story of how her own mother gave her the recipe as part of her bridal trousseau. This recipe is part of her family tradition.

5 eggs

1 tsp vanilla extract, or 2 tsp rose water

1 tsp baking powder

3¼ cups (485 g) flour

vegetable oil for deep-frying

1½ cups (165 g) slivered almonds, toasted

1½ cups (225 g) whole hazelnuts, toasted

1 cup (250 mL) honey

1 cup (200 g) granulated sugar

In a mixing bowl, beat eggs, then add vanilla and baking powder. Mix until smooth. Stir in flour and knead into soft and pliable dough, adding more flour if necessary.

Pinch off a walnut-sized piece of dough and roll on a flat surface into a thin rope approximately ½ in (1 cm) wide, then cut into pea-sized pieces. Cover balls with a tea towel as you go, until all dough has been formed into balls.

In a saucepan on medium, heat enough oil for deep-frying. Deep-fry dough balls for 2 minutes or until light golden brown. Remove with a slotted spoon and drain on paper towel, then place in a large mixing bowl. Add almonds and hazelnuts and mix well.

Continues...

In a medium saucepan on medium heat, add honey and stir in sugar until all the sugar is dissolved. Cook, stirring continuously, until honey begins to boil. Continue cooking until honey froths and rises about ¾ up the saucepan. Remove from heat and stir to bring down froth. Immediately pour hot honey onto fried dough and nuts and stir to coat.

Pour mixture onto a large buttered serving platter and pat down evenly. Let cool, then cut into individual portions or break off into bite-sized pieces.

MAKES 12 TO 14 SERVINGS

Qataayif 'Asafeeree

Bird-Size Stuffed Pancakes

Qataayif are one of the oldest traditional Syrian sweets. No one can say they have visited Damascus until they have tasted these crepe-like pancakes filled with nuts, cheese, or in this case, *qashta*, a thick, sweet custard similar to clotted cream, and drizzled with sugar syrup flavored with rose water or orange blossom water. Their elegant appearance is nothing compared to their taste—totally irresistible! This has been a steady sentiment since the Middle Ages, when the scholar Abu Bakr ibn al-Arabi gave these sweets the title *lafaa'if al-na'eem*, or Rolls of Bliss.

Qashta

¾ cup (95 g) cornstarch

3 cups (700 mL) whole milk, divided

¾ cup (180 g) heavy cream

3 tbsp sugar

2 tbsp rose water

2 tbsp orange blossom water

Pancakes

½ cup (75 g) flour

½ cup (100 g) fine semolina

3 tbsp sugar

1 tsp baking powder

½ tsp active dry yeast

pinch of salt

1 tsp rose water

2½ cups (625 mL) warm water

½ cup (50 g) finely chopped pistachios

¼ cup (60 mL) *qatr* (see p. 69)

Continues...

For the *qashta:* In a mixing bowl, combine cornstarch and ¾ cup (175 mL) milk. Stir until smooth, making sure there are no lumps.

In a saucepan on medium-low heat, stir together remaining milk and cream. Add sugar and mix well. Stir in rose water and orange blossom water, mixing well. Keep stirring until heated through, almost hot to the touch.

Add cornstarch-milk mixture to saucepan contents and keep stirring on medium-low heat until thick and bubbly.

Remove from heat, pour into a bowl, and let cool. Mixture will thicken as it cools. Refrigerate for 2 hours, or until ready to use. *Qashta* covered with plastic wrap will keep in the refrigerator for 1 week.

For the pancakes: In a mixing bowl, combine flour, semolina, sugar, baking powder, yeast, and salt. Stir in water and rose water, then whisk well so that there are no lumps. Cover and let sit for 30 minutes.

Heat a griddle to 350°F (180°C) or a nonstick frying pan to medium. Spray lightly with cooking spray.

With a small ladle (about 2 tbsp) pour batter in a 2-in (5-cm) circle. Cook until bubbles form on the top and the bottom is cooked, golden, and dry. DO NOT FLIP OVER. Remove and place on a tray uncooked side up. Cover with plastic wrap to prevent drying out. Repeat with remaining batter.

For the stuffing: One modern method is to pipe the *qashta* into the partially closed pancake. However, we went with the traditional way of using a spoon. Take a pancake in your hand and fold it into a half circle and pinch it closed halfway. Gently spoon 1 tsp of *qashta* into the open end. Dip open side with the filling into pistachios. Arrange *qataayif* on a serving platter and drizzle with syrup.

MAKES 25 PANCAKES

Halaawat al-Jibn

Stuffed Sweet Cheese Rolls

In restaurants and at homes of friends and relatives in Syria, we were served a dish of four or more *halaawat al-jibn* with a knife and fork. Upon our return home, we opted to eat this dessert with our fingers instead.

Halaawat al-jibn are rolls of cheese dough stuffed with *qashta* (see p. 309), a thick, sweet custard-cream. A lot of muscle is needed to stir the cheese to get the correct texture for the dough. So make sure you've had a good night's sleep and are ready to face the vigorous beating of cheese and semolina.

½ recipe *qatr* (see p. 69), divided

½ cup (125 mL) water

4 tbsp sugar

1 8-oz (226-g) package shredded mozzarella cheese

½ cup (100 g) fine semolina

2 tbsp orange blossom water

½ recipe *qashta* (see p. 309)

¼ cup (25 g) ground pistachios

Flatten a piece of heavy plastic wrap over the countertop (or you can do this directly on the counter if you don't mind cleaning up the syrup after!). Pour ¼ cup (30 g) *qatr* on the plastic and spread evenly.

In a sturdy saucepan on medium heat, mix water and sugar using a wooden spoon. Stir until it comes to a boil. Stir in cheese and keep stirring until sugar water is incorporated into cheese and becomes a heavy mass.

Gradually add semolina, whisking and beating strongly with every addition, ensuring semolina is incorporated into cheese. Quickly beat in orange blossom water until blended.

Transfer the cheese ball immediately to the *qatr*-coated plastic. Quickly use your fingers to flatten the ball into a ⅛-in (3-mm) thick rectangle. If dough

Continues...

is too hot to touch, wet your fingertips with a little cold water. Trim uneven edges to maintain the rectangle shape. You can re-shape the offcuts into another rectangle.

Spoon *qashta* in an even line along the long, bottom edge of the cheese rectangle. Begin to roll the plastic with the cheese dough over the *qashta*. Continue to carefully roll the cheese dough, pressing slightly and ensuring the filling is wrapped in the dough with one complete roll. repeat process with remaining cheese dough. Cut along the line of the plastic, remove the rolled, stuffed cheese cylinder, and set aside. Repeat the process with the remaining cheese dough.

With a sharp knife, cut rolls on a diagonal into slices 1½ in (4 cm) wide. Place on a serving platter. Garnish with pistachios and drizzle with *qatr*. Cover with plastic wrap and refrigerate for at least 1 hour before serving.

MAKES 30 TO 35 ROLLS

Hajjee Baba

Cherried Bread

This traditional cherry dessert from Aleppo is usually made with a base of dried biscuits or a type of biscotti. But our dear friend the late Hind Jabri made us this version one evening, and we fell in love with the delicious buttery bread infused with a rich, fruity syrup. Traditionally, Aleppo cherries should be used, but they are very difficult to find outside the city. We use canned cherries, but black currants can also be substituted.

8 tbsp butter

1 baguette sliced into 12 rounds, about 1¼ in (3 cm) thick

1 4½ oz (411-g) can pitted tart red cherries, packed in water

¾ cup (150 g) sugar

In a frying pan on medium heat, melt butter and brown bread rounds on both sides, for 2 minutes or until deep golden. Transfer to a serving plate.

In a small saucepan on high heat, bring cherries and their water with sugar to a boil. Reduce heat to medium and cook for 10 minutes, stirring occasionally. Then whisk saucepan contents and cook for a further 10 minutes, whisking often.

Remove from heat. With a hand mixer, blend cherries until mixture thickens. Let cool and pass the mixture through a sieve into a bowl to make cherry sauce.

Dip each piece of bread into sauce, coating all sides, or spoon sauce over bread, and place in a serving bowl.

MAKES 4 SERVINGS

Almaaseeya

Diamond Pudding

Almaaseeya means diamond-like—a fitting name for this clear and sparkling Jell-O–like pudding that resembles a beautifully cut jewel. Light and refreshing, with the distinct flavor of rose water, *almaaseeya* is more commonly made with milk, which results in a shiny white pudding. However, our recipe without milk has been handed down from great-grandmother to grandmother to mother to daughters.

2 tbsp ground pistachios, divided

½ cup (65 g) cornstarch

4½ cups (1.1 L) cold water, divided

¾ cup (150 g) sugar

1½ tbsp rose water

½ recipe *qatr* using rose water (see p. 69)

Prepare a Bundt pan for the *almaaseeya* by moistening it slightly with water. Sprinkle 1 tbsp pistachios around the inside of the mold.

In a mixing bowl, combine cornstarch and 1 cup (250 mL) water. Stir well, making sure there are no lumps.

In a deep saucepan on medium-high heat, bring remaining water to a boil. Add cornstarch mixture, stirring constantly until it comes to a boil. Reduce heat to medium-low, stirring continuously, and simmer for 30 minutes until mixture thickens.

Stir in sugar until dissolved, then stir in rose water. Pour mixture into the mold. The mold should be deep enough for the *almaaseeya* to reach the top.

Refrigerate overnight.

Invert the mold onto a serving dish and sprinkle pudding with remaining pistachios. Slice into individual portions and drizzle *qatr* according to taste.

MAKES 6 TO 8 SERVINGS

Balouza

Damascene Milk Pudding

This rich dessert is prepared almost the same way as *almaaseeya* (see p. 314) but is a little more colorful and elaborate. There's just something about apricots and cream that brings back memories of beautiful Damascus.

6 tbsp cornstarch, divided

2 cups (500 mL) whole milk, divided

½ cup (100 g) + 2 tbsp sugar

½ tsp rose water

1 tbsp orange blossom water

2 tbsp ground almonds, toasted

2 tbsp ground pistachios

½ cup (125 mL) water, divided

4 tbsp finely chopped dried apricots

1 tbsp unsalted butter

2 tbsp orange juice (fresh-squeezed is best), or a pinch of saffron mixed with 2 tbsp water

whipped cream (optional)

pistachios, coarsely ground (optional)

In a saucepan on medium heat, mix 4 tbsp cornstarch with 1 cup (250 mL) milk. Stir in remaining milk, ½ cup (100 g) sugar, rose water, and orange blossom water, making sure all ingredients are blended well. Cook, stirring continuously, until mixture thickens to the consistency of smooth pudding. Remove from heat and stir in almonds and pistachios. Spoon mixture into 6 serving cups and refrigerate for 1 hour.

In a saucepan on medium-low heat, combine ¼ cup (60 mL) water, apricots, and butter. Cook, stirring continuously, until there are no lumps and apricots have become a thick paste. Remove from heat and stir in remaining 2 tbsp sugar and orange juice or diluted saffron.

In a small bowl, mix remaining water and cornstarch, then stir into apricot paste. Return paste to medium-low heat and stir continuously until mixture thickens, about 10 minutes. Remove from heat.

Evenly spoon apricot mixture over chilled pudding and refrigerate for 1 hour. Serve immediately as is or topped with whipped cream sprinkled with ground pistachios.

MAKES 6 SERVINGS

Ma'mouneeya

Semolina Pudding Fit for a Caliph

It is said that this regal dish named after the 9th-century caliph al-Ma'mun was brought by travelers and merchants from Baghdad to Aleppo, where it developed into the specialty of the city. This velvety smooth semolina pudding is typically made on Fridays, the day off from work for Syrians, when families gather and enjoy a good-morning treat. This is Habeeb's version—less sweet but much tastier. Serve this with hot bread and cheese to complement the pudding's sweetness and velvety texture.

4 tbsp butter

1 cup (200 g) fine semolina

1 cup (250 mL) milk

1 cup (200 g) sugar

1 cup (120 g) *qashta* (see p. 309) or 1 cup (120 g) whipped cream

4 tbsp crushed pistachios

cinnamon (optional)

In a saucepan on medium heat, melt butter and stir-fry semolina for 3 to 5 minutes or until golden. Reduce heat to low, stir in milk and sugar, then stir for 10 minutes or until semolina is a soft paste, adding a little water if necessary.

Spread on a platter and allow to set for 15 minutes.

Spread *qashta* or whipped cream evenly over top. Sprinkle with pistachios and a little cinnamon, if desired.

MAKES 8 SERVINGS

Ruzz bil-Haleeb

Syrian Rice Pudding

This dessert is the Syrian way of "puttin' on the *ruzz*"—few others can boast such guilt-free enjoyment of something sweet. It is quick and easy to make and a favorite food for children. For variety, add toppings such as toasted coconut, pine nuts, walnuts, almonds, and even caramel or cinnamon.

1 cup (250 mL) water	¼ cup (40 g) raisins
¼ cup (50 g) basmati or any other long-grain white rice, rinsed	¼ cup (50 g) sugar
	1 tbsp cornstarch
	1 tsp almond extract
1 cup (250 mL) light cream	2 tbsp chopped pistachios
1 cup (250 mL) whole milk	

In a saucepan, bring water and rice to a boil. Reduce heat to medium, cook for 10 minutes, then add remaining ingredients except pistachios and bring to a boil. Reduce heat to medium and cook for 10 minutes, stirring constantly.

Place in serving cups, let sit for 10 minutes, then refrigerate for 1 hour. Sprinkle with pistachios and serve.

MAKES 8 SERVINGS

Raa'ihat al-Rummaan bi-Maa' Ward

The Scent of Pomegranates and Rose Water

When the Umayyads were defeated by the Abbasids in 750 CE in Damascus, only one member of the Umayyad family survived and escaped to the Iberian Peninsula. Abd al-Rahman I could never return home, so to soothe his homesickness, his sister sent him the most famous variety of Syrian pomegranate, the Rusafa. The fruit flourished in his lavish gardens, and the emir had the scent of Damascus always within his reach. For our family, Fareeda would make this fragrant dessert on special occasions, especially when her grandchildren came over, and she would tell them about this ancient city, her family's city. Her memory is forever associated with the scent of pomegranates and rose water.

In the 18th century, it was not unusual to be presented with cut pomegranates or saucers of pomegranate seeds sprinkled with sugar and rose water at the dining table.

seeds from 4 large pomegranates
½ cup (70 g) pine nuts
½ cup (65 g) coarsely chopped
   walnuts

4 tbsp sugar
1 tbsp rose water

In a bowl, thoroughly mix all ingredients, then place in a serving bowl or individual cups and chill for 1 hour.

MAKES 4 TO 6 SERVINGS

Drinks

· · · · · · · · · ·

Qahwa 'Arabeeya

Arab Coffee

While on a visit to the ancient oasis city of Palmyra in the Syrian Desert, we decided to enjoy a cup of Arab coffee in the designated coffee room in the lobby of our hotel, the Zenobia Cham Palace. The manager proudly explained that the symbolism of Syrian coffee is threefold: its rich aroma signifies the joy of meeting, its bitterness represents the sadness of parting, and its blackness evokes the dark eyes of the beloved.

2 heaping tbsp pulverized Arab coffee (or dark roast or espresso)

1 tbsp sugar
2 cups (500 mL) water
1 cardamom seed, crushed

In a saucepan on medium-high heat, bring coffee, sugar, and water to a boil. When coffee begins to froth, remove from heat. Stir in cardamom and return to heat until froth rises again. Remove from heat and allow coffee to settle for 1 minute, then spoon a little froth into each demitasse cup. Pour in coffee and serve immediately.

MAKES 4 DEMITASSE CUPS

Shaay Souree

Syrian Tea

Shaay aswad—black tea—is considered the national drink of Syria. It is also called *shaay ahmar*, because of the tea's reddish tinge. Breakfast is incomplete without freshly baked Arab bread and a glass of hot black tea. Guests are always offered tea (or coffee), and in a gesture of hospitality, many businesses serve their customers tea made in-house. Arab tea is traditionally made using a *breek*, a type of pitcher that can handle the heat of a gas or electric stove. It is then strained into a teapot and served. But we have simply used a saucepan. Syrians like their tea strong, just like their country.

5 cups (1.25 L) water   3 tbsp black tea leaves
5 tbsp sugar

In a saucepan, bring water and sugar to a boil, remove from heat, then add tea leaves. Let sit for 5 minutes. If the tea sits too long before serving, bitterness sets in, and if not long enough, then it is too weak. Pour through a strainer into a teapot and serve immediately in small tea glasses.

MAKES 10 3-OZ (90-ML) TEA GLASSES

Shaay bil-Yansoun

Aniseed Tea

> There are some who wonder why Arab tea and coffee are served in small glasses or cups. Some may say that both are strong brews and a little goes a long way. However, we believe that because hospitality is so important in Syria—in all Arab culture—visitors are served small glasses or cups so that they can ask for more and thus stay longer as honored guests.

This sweet tea, lightly spiced with anise, is often prepared for someone who feels something coming on, or is downright under the weather. Many Syrian mothers use it for gripe water. You can make it *bi-doun sukkar* (without sugar) if you want it unsweetened.

4 tsp aniseed

5 tbsp sugar

2½ cups (625 mL) water

4 tbsp loose black tea

3½ cups (830 mL) boiling water

chopped walnuts or slivered blanched almonds for garnish

In a saucepan, mix aniseed and sugar. Pour in 2 ½ cups (625 mL) water and bring to a boil. Reduce heat to medium-low and simmer for 10 minutes. Reduce heat to low and keep warm.

Put tea leaves in a tea infuser in a large teapot and pour in 3 ½ cups (830 mL) boiling water. Let sit for 2 minutes, then remove tea infuser.

Pour anise mixture through a strainer into the teapot. Pour tea into demi-tasse tea glasses and garnish with nuts. Serve immediately.

MAKES 10 TO 12 3-OZ (90-ML) TEA GLASSES

Mighlee

Spicy Syrian Tisane

Mighlee is also the name of a spiced pudding usually referred to as *karaweeya* (caraway) in Syria. This slow-cooked rice pudding also features cinnamon and aniseed, with the addition of caraway. It is decorated with walnuts, pine nuts, pistachios, and, frequently, toasted coconut. According to folklore, the pudding's light brown color represents fertile soil for the "birth" of a new growing season.

Syrians celebrate the birth of a baby, including the birth of Jesus at Christmas, with cups of hot and spicy *mighlee*. The floating nuts make *mighlee* extra delicious and add crunch.

8 tsp walnut halves, divided
8 tsp pine nuts, divided
8 tsp slivered almonds, divided
4 cups (1 L) water
6 tsp sugar

1 tbsp aniseed
2 3-in (8-cm) cinnamon sticks
4 cloves
¼ tsp nutmeg
1 tbsp grated ginger

In 4 teacups, place 2 tsp each of walnuts, pine nuts, and almonds and set aside.

In a saucepan, add water, then stir in sugar until it dissolves. Bring to a boil, then add remaining ingredients. Reduce heat to medium-low, cover, and simmer for 10 minutes. Strain and pour into the cups over the nuts. Serve immediately.

MAKES 4 CUPS (1 L)

Sharaab Dibs Rummaan

Pomegranate Drink

Thirst-quenching and refreshing, this drink is a must during an afternoon siesta on a hot day. We have added fresh pomegranate seeds for a fruitier flavor and a bit of crunch.

4 cups (1 L) water

1 tbsp rose water

½ cup (125 mL) *dibs rummaan*

sugar to taste

4 tsp fresh pomegranate seeds

Combine all ingredients except pomegranate seeds. Pour into 4 glasses, then stir 1 tsp pomegranate seeds into each. Add ice cubes and serve immediately.

MAKES 4 SERVINGS

Laymounaada

Lemon and Mint Slush

Nothing is more refreshing than a glass of lemonade. But a slightly sweet, minty lemon slush is even better.

4 large lemons, ends removed

4 cups (144 g) ice cubes

1 cup (200 g) sugar

2 tbsp orange blossom water

1 cup (250 mL) cold water

⅔ cup (22 g) mint leaves

lemon slices

Cut lemons in quarters, leaving on the rind but removing the seeds. In a food processor or blender, mix lemon with remaining ingredients for 2 minutes (the amount of sugar and orange blossom water can be adjusted according to taste), until mixture is the consistency of a thin slushy, and pour over ice. Garnish with fresh mint and lemon slices.

MAKES 6 GOBLETS

Sharaab Qamar al-Deen

Apricot Drink

One of the most popular beverages served to break the Ramadan fast is this one made from *qamar al-deen*, which explains why its name translates to "the moon of religion." *Qamar al-deen* are sheets of dried apricot paste, similar to a Fruit Roll-Up. Since medieval times, Syria has been known for the best-quality and tastiest apricots, especially those from the groves of the Ghouta around Damascus. Dried apricot paste is available in Arab groceries or the international section of supermarkets.

2 cups (380 g) *qamar al-deen,* cut into small pieces

boiling water

5 cups (1.25 L) water

5 tbsp sugar

orange blossom water (optional)

In a deep bowl, cover *qamar al-deen* with 1 in (2.5 cm) boiling water. Cover and let sit for 3 hours, or until *qamar al-deen* is dissolved, stirring occasionally. Strain through a sieve into a bowl and whisk in 5 cups (1.25 L) water and sugar. Pour into a pitcher and refrigerate for 1 hour. Serve chilled or over ice. Add a few drops of orange blossom water if desired.

MAKES 6 GOBLETS

Jullaab

Julep

This syrup made from grape molasses, carob, dates, and rose water has a long history. In medieval Damascus, the favorite drink was diluted rose water syrup known as *jullaab*, chilled with ice. One of the most refreshing summertime drinks in Syria, and one of the easiest to make, *jullaab* is an invigorating and revitalizing way to beat the heat. But not to worry—you can enjoy it all year long.

1¼ cups (310 mL) cold water

2 tbsp *jullaab*

1 tsp pine nuts

1 tsp chopped walnuts

1 tsp golden raisins

Mix together all ingredients in a large glass. Add crushed ice or ice cubes and enjoy!

MAKES 1 1/2 CUPS (375 ML)

The word "julep" meaning "sweetened water" came into Middle English via Middle French, which took it from the Arabic *jullaab*. The word originates from the Persian *gulāb*, which is a combination of *gul* (rose) and *āb* (water).

Shaneena

Yogurt Drink

In yogurt-loving Syria, this simple and nutritious beverage is popular with young and old.

5 cups (1.25 L) 3% (whole milk) yogurt

3 cups (700 mL) water

1 tsp salt

dried mint (optional)

In a blender, combine all ingredients except mint and blend for 1 minute. Transfer to a pitcher and refrigerate until needed. Serve over crushed ice. Sprinkle each serving with dried mint if desired.

MAKES 8 SERVINGS

Acknowledgments

We wish to thank our friends and colleagues Samira Helbaoui, the late Hind Jabri, Leila Kronfol, Najah Dayoub, and Kamal Salibi for their advice about some of the recipes in this book, especially those that had no previous written records. Their resources were family experiences, history, and the traditions in which they, like us, were raised. And within this scope of Syrian tradition, we realize the importance of recording for posterity the dishes that Syrians have been raised on, lived with, and enjoyed for centuries. It is for the sake of continuity and acknowledging our past that we offer these recipes to the world of gastronomy, a world that appears to be void of these special Syrian dishes.

Also, we wish to thank the many Syrians with whom we discussed some of the dishes and their traditions during our numerous trips to Syria. Their insight into a class of dishes, almost lost to history, proved invaluable in our pursuit of learning, cooking, and presentation.

Further, we acknowledge family, friends, and colleagues who offered their opinions about the dishes we prepared. They took on the task of tasting with gusto; proud to learn about dishes from an ancient land. Then, of course, there is Issam Elias, who diligently added nuance to the translations of old recipes where needed.

In addition, we wish to thank those writers and journalists from the mid-18th to the early 20th centuries, as well as more recent authors whose books and articles widened our horizons about Syrian food. The authors who traveled in Greater Syria in the 18th and 19th centuries, and recorded their observations of the society, people, and culture, such as Alexander Russell in *The Natural History of Aleppo* (1794) and John Lewis Burckhardt in *Travels in Syria and the Holy Land* (1822), gave us insight into what people ate and what ingredients were available then. Newspaper articles, such as the ones that appeared in the *New York Times*, *Herald and News*, *News and Citizen*, and *New York Sun* from 1889 to 1905, covered what Syrians ate at home and served in their small restaurants in the Syrian quarters provide an insight into the traditional dishes that immigrants brought with them. The descriptions of some of these dishes helped us decipher what was used and how they were made. Paul Strathern's *Napoleon in Egypt* (2008) and James D. Grehan's detailed *Everyday Life and Consumer Culture in 18th-Century Damascus* (2007) are valuable studies in the history of Greater Syria.

The poetry excerpt by Ishaq al-Mawsili on pages 10–11 is from *Kitab al-Tabikh*, compiled by Ibn Sayyar al-Warraq, edited by Kaj Öhrnberg and Sahban Mroueh, and published by the Finnish Oriental Society, 1987, page 90. It was translated by Muna Salloum and Leila Salloum Elias.

Arabic sources provided intrinsic and elaborate descriptions of many of the region's traditional dishes. Articles written by Arab food historians and interviews with old-timers well versed in the hands-on preparation of these dishes gave us a better understanding of what and why we enjoy what we eat.

Finally, a great word of thanks to our parents and our grandparents and theirs as well, for had they not kept the traditions and taste of Syrian cooking on our breakfast, lunch, and dinner tables, we would not have had this culinary tradition available to us today. Foremost, Shams, mother to Habeeb and grandmother to Leila and Muna, and Nabeeha, mother to Fareeda, and grandmother to Leila and Muna, who brought their Syrian, especially their Damascene recipes with them.

Finally, we acknowledge Fareeda Abourezk Salloum, late wife, mother and grandmother who was a first-generation Syrian Canadian, born in Canada. She set the table with her beautiful Syrian dishes and preserved the essence of these dishes from the old world in the new.

—Habeeb Salloum
Leila Salloum Elias
Muna Salloum

Index

Page numbers in italics refer to photographs.

About the Authors

HABEEB SALLOUM was born in the Qaraoun, Syria, and emigrated to Canada as an infant. Habeeb, alongside his daughters, **LEILA SALLOUM ELIAS** (Arabic instructor, Penn State University) and **MUNA SALLOUM** (business manager, University of Toronto) have co-authored more than 10 books, including: *The Arabian Nights Cookbook, Scheherazade's Feasts, Arab Cooking on a Prairie Homestead* (winner of the Cuisine Canada Award), *From the Lands of Figs and Olives*, and *Sweet Delights from a Thousand and One Nights*.

For the last 25 years, Habeeb has been a freelance writer and author, specializing in food, history, and travel. He's published articles in the *Toronto Star*, the *Globe and Mail*, the *Western Producer, Contemporary Review, Vegetarian Journal*, and *Saveur*. He contributed a chapter on the history of the Syrians in Canada to the *Encyclopedia of Canada's Peoples*.

Partial proceeds from the sale of this book will benefit Le centre culturel syrien (Syrian Cultural Centre), a nonprofit organization based in Montreal currently dedicating its efforts to help alleviate the plight of the displaced and those who have been impacted by the situation in Syria.

centreculturelsyrien.org